The Power of Assessment for Learning

The Power of Assessment for Learning

Twenty Years of Research and Practice in UK and US Classrooms

Margaret Heritage and Christine Harrison
Foreword by Dylan Wiliam

CORWIN
A SAGE Publishing Company

A SAGE Publishing Company

FOR INFORMATION:

Corwin

A SAGE Company

2455 Teller Road

Thousand Oaks, California 91320

(800) 233-9936

www.corwin.com

SAGE Publications Ltd.

1 Oliver's Yard

55 City Road

London EC1Y 1SP

United Kingdom

SAGE Publications India Pvt. Ltd.

B 1/I 1 Mohan Cooperative Industrial Area

Mathura Road, New Delhi 110 044

India

SAGE Publications Asia-Pacific Pte. Ltd.

18 Cross Street #10-10/11/12

China Square Central

Singapore 048423

Program Director: Jessica Allan

Content Development Editor: Lucas Schleicher

Senior Editorial Assistant: Mia Rodriguez

Production Editor: Tori Mirsadjadi

Copy Editor: Amy Hanquist Harris

Typesetter: Hurix Digital

Proofreader: Barbara Coster

Indexer: Maria Sosnowski

Cover Designer: Lysa Becker

Marketing Manager: Deena Meyer

Printed in the United States of America.

Library of Congress Cataloging-in-Publication Data

Names: Heritage, Margaret, author. | Harrison, Christine (Christine Ann), author.

Title: The power of assessment for learning : twenty years of research and practice in US and UK classrooms / Margaret Heritage and Christine Harrison ; foreword by Dylan William.

Description: First edition. | Thousand Oaks, California : Corwin, 2020. | Includes bibliographical references.

Identifiers: LCCN 2019030334 | ISBN 9781544361468 (paperback) | ISBN 9781544394084 (epub) | ISBN 9781544394169 (epub) | ISBN 9781544394213 (ebook)

Subjects: LCSH: Educational evaluation—United States. | Educational tests and measurements—United States. | Effective teaching—United States. | Educational evaluation—Great Britain. | Educational tests and measurements—Great Britain. | Effective teaching—Great Britian.

Classification: LCC LB3051 .H4443 2020 | DDC 371.26—dc23 LC record available at https://lccn.loc.gov/2019030334

This book is printed on acid-free paper.

19 20 21 22 23 10 9 8 7 6 5 4 3 2 1

Contents

Foreword

••

by Dylan Wiliam

Looking back over the quarter century or so in which I have been research-ing and writing about formative assessment, I am struck by a number of things.

The first is that the idea that teachers should use evidence about stu-dent achievement to inform and adjust their instruction seems, in retro-spect, so obvious that it is surprising that anyone needed to point this out at all. Over fifty years ago, in his earliest work on mastery learning, Benjamin Bloom pointed out that many teachers treated instruction as a linear process. Teachers taught and students understood the material to a greater or lesser extent, producing a range of achievement. Drawing on the work of John Carroll, Bloom suggested that we should think of the notion of aptitude not as the proportion of what they were taught that students remembered, but the time students took to reach a level of mastery. From such a perspective, the traditional bell curve was a sign of instructional failure: "In fact, we may even insist that our educational efforts have been unsuccessful to the extent to which our distribution of achievement approximates the normal distribution" (Bloom, 1968, p. 3). Because what students learned from instruction was not predictable, teachers needed to find out what the students had actually learned before deciding what to do next. Teaching became a contingent, rather than a linear process.

Of course, even this was not entirely new. Many of the individual-ized approaches to instruction such as Frederic Burk's individual plan (Reiser, 1986), the Dalton Plan (Parkhurst, 1922), and the Winnetka Plan (Washburne, 1941) in the United States, as well as the Kent Mathemat-ics Project in the United Kingdom (Banks, 1991), had been based on the idea that teachers should use assessment on a regular basis to decide next instructional steps. In the early 1980s, American educator Madeline Hunter had stressed the need for "frequent checks of understanding" dur-ing teaching (Hunter, 1982, pp. 59–62) and so the review that Paul Black and I published in 1998 was in many senses just a confirmation of the power of assessment to improve learning that had been at the heart of good educators' practice for decades, if not centuries.

What was, perhaps, original about our review was that we collected a wide range of evidence about the impact of such practices on learning and, as Margaret and Chris point out in Chapter 1, our work helped organize research studies from a number of different fields. Rather than trying to synthesize the research through a meta-analysis, we were more concerned to make sense of the research—what David Gough (2015) has termed a configurative, rather than an aggregative review. In addition, by collecting the relevant research evidence in one place, we showed that teachers did not have to choose between teaching well and raising test scores—teaching well was the best way to raise test scores.

A second thing that strikes me, looking back over the last twenty-five years, is that it has proven to be much harder than we imagined to support teachers in developing their formative assessment practice. Part of this, no doubt, is due to the policy environments in place in both the US and the UK at the time that the authors describe in Chapter 2. Part also is surely due to cultural assumptions about the respective role of teachers and students in classrooms, and, especially in the context of assessment, involving students in peer and self-assessment seems to many somewhat akin to letting the fox guard the henhouse, or letting the lunatics run the asylum. These responses just show how far the summative function of assessment dominates thinking in most educational systems. As Chris and Margaret show in Chapter 3, involving students, both as owners of their own learning and as learning resources for one another, suggests profound changes in assumptions about how schools should work.

A third thing that is clear in retrospect, but which was not clear (or at least not clear enough) when we began this work, is that for all but the least experienced teachers, developing formative assessment is primarily a process of habit change, and not one of knowledge acquisition. There is a substantial body of research on habit change, especially in health education, but for many years we had not realized how central this research would be to our work with teachers. As the authors point out in Chapter 4, we had always understood that the development of formative assessment practice involved more than just adding a few techniques to teachers' routines, but instead, involved deep changes in teachers' practice. But I think we underestimated just how profound the changes needed were, especially in countries like the US and the UK, where teachers are routinely expected to be in front of their students for twenty-two to twenty-five hours each week.

And that is why this book represents such an important contribution to our thinking about the use of assessment in instruction. To the casual observer, the title of the book might suggest that it is a retrospective—a history of twenty years of attempts to develop the use of assessment in instruction in both the UK and the US. And of course in one sense, it is that. But it is also much more. By looking at the difficulties that have been encountered in supporting teachers in developing their formative assessment practice, by understanding how policy environments and cultural considerations make it more or less difficult to support teachers in developing their practice, Chris and Margaret provide, in Chapter 5, a clear blueprint on how to take this work forward.

Of course this will be far from straightforward. In Chapter 6, the authors identify a number of issues that will need further exploration as we try to harness the power of assessment to improve learning, and we do need more work on the role of disciplinary knowledge, learner identities, and so on. But this is not the researcher's lament of "more research is needed." More research is, of course, always needed, but as this book shows, while the evidence is never as good as we would like it to be, there is now overwhelming evidence that attention to classroom assessment processes has to be part of any serious attempt to improve educational outcomes for young people, and the advice contained in this book provides a clear guide for action for educators, not just in the US and the UK, but all over the world.

REFERENCES

Banks, B. (1991). *The KMP way to learn maths: A history of the early development of the Kent Mathematics Project*. Maidstone, UK: Bertram Banks.

Bloom, B. S. (1968). Learning for mastery. *Evaluation Comment, 1*(2), 1–12.

Gough, D. (2015). Qualitative and mixed methods in systematic reviews. *Systematic Reviews, 4*(181), 1–3. doi: 10.1186/s13643–015–0151-y

Hunter, M. C. (1982). *Mastery teaching*. El Segundo, CA: Tip Publications.

Parkhurst, H. (1922). *Education on the Dalton Plan*. London, UK: G. Bell and Sons, Ltd.

Reiser, R. A. (1986). Instructional technology: A history. In R. M. Gagné (Ed.), *Instructional technology: Foundations* (pp. 11–48). Hillsdale, NJ: Lawrence Erlbaum Associates.

Washburne, C. (1941). *A living philosophy of education*. Chicago, IL: University of Chicago Press.

Preface

● ●

Just over twenty years ago, two British researchers, Paul Black and Dylan Wiliam, published their now-famous review on assessment for learning (AfL), primarily known as formative assessment in the United States. Their review was initially commissioned by the Assessment Reform Group in response to a concern among scholars and educators about the increasing influence of large-scale summative assessment in the United Kingdom on teaching and learning. Teachers were focusing on summative results while ongoing assessment of student learning was receiving scant attention.

Black and Wiliam published their extensive review first in an academic journal (1998a) and subsequently in a practitioner-friendly version as *Inside the Black Box* (1998b). Their review was not the first of its kind. Previously, New Zealand scholar Terry Crooks had written a review in 1988 summarizing results from fourteen specific fields of research that cast light on the relationships between classroom assessment practices and student outcomes. Crooks paid particular attention to learning strategies, motivation, and achievement. The conclusions he derived from these specific fields were then merged into an integrated summary, spelling out assessment's powerful direct and indirect impacts on classroom practice. Crooks noted that classroom assessment affects students in many different ways: It guides their judgment of what is important to learn, affects their motivation and self-perceptions of competence, structures their approaches to personal study, and affects the development of enduring learning strategies and skills. He concluded that assessment appears to be one of the most potent forces influencing education. Accordingly, it deserves very careful planning and considerable investment of time from educators.

Ten years later, Black and Wiliam's review established AfL as an explicit domain of assessment practice. Comprising diverse bodies of research, including classroom discourse practices, student self-perception, and teachers' assessment practices, their review concluded that formative assessment is a game changer: Implementing AfL can lead to significant learning gains (Black & Wiliam, 1998a). Since 1998, the extent of the effect on achievement that Black and Wiliam described has been challenged (e.g., Kingston & Nash, 2011). However, available evidence indicates that considerable improvements in student achievement are possible—even likely—when teachers implement AfL routinely and frequently (e.g., Andersson & Palm, 2017; Brown & Harris, 2013; Hattie & Timperley, 2007; Wiliam, Lee, Harrison, & Black, 2004).

In their review, Black and Wiliam (1998c) defined *formative assessment* as "encompassing all those activities undertaken by teachers, and/or by students, which provide information to be used as feedback to modify the teaching and learning activities in which they are engaged" (p. 7).

In the two decades or so since their review, research, theory, and practice have expanded conceptions of assessment for learning—for instance, placing AfL as part of daily classroom practice is more explicit (Cowie, 2005; Harrison, 2015; Heritage, 2010; Willis, 2007), the role of students in the assessment process and the associated development of their self-regulation skills is receiving increased emphasis (e.g., Bailey & Heritage, 2018), and the importance of disciplinary considerations in implementing assessment for learning is gaining ground (Andrade, Bennett, & Cizek, 2019; Shepard, Penuel, & Pellegrino, 2018). AfL has also expanded the role of feedback in the formative process, emphasizing the importance of feedback from students to teachers as the main driver of next steps in learning because it provides teachers with sufficient evidence to make pedagogical decisions about whether to move ideas forward or to fill gaps in knowledge or skills.

Black and Wiliam's review stimulated worldwide interest, resulting in AfL being taken up in countries from New Zealand to Pakistan to Ethiopia. This book aims to tell the story of formative assessment in two specific countries: the UK and the US. Our purpose is threefold: (1) to mark the twentieth anniversary of Black and Wiliam's landmark review and reassert the importance and value of AfL; (2) to trace its journey of implementation in two very different education systems, comparing and contrasting changes in conceptions and practice across both countries and evaluating the benefits that have accrued to teaching and learning in each; and (3) to consider future developments in growing and sustaining AfL practice.

Throughout the book, it will be evident that the two education systems use different terms to refer to the same thing. As far as possible, we have endeavored to clarify the differences in terms. We should note that we have chosen to use the term *AfL*, which has its genesis in the UK, rather than the term *formative assessment*, which is more common in the US. This is because AfL as a set of practices came to prominence in the UK as a result of Black and Wiliam's review and because, in our view, it reflects more strongly the idea that this assessment process is part of ongoing teaching and learning rather than as a test event, which the term *formative assessment* can still conjure up for some educators. References to "formative assessment**s**" (suggesting specific tests rather than ongoing assessment during teaching and learning) are still quite common in the US.

Now we turn to our personal stories of how we came to write this book.

Christine's Story

I taught science for thirteen years in and around London, and this experience showed me how important it was to get assessment right. I remember teaching the topic of hard water to 12-year-old students for three weeks, and at the end of that period, I gave them a test. I was horrified to find that many of my students had given many incorrect answers; yet their notes in their books and their responses in my lessons suggested they had understood the topic. I decided to ask them what they thought hard water was, and I was mortified when one student asked, "Is it ice?" We had done various experiments on hard and soft water to illustrate their different properties, and I had shown the students lime scale in kettles and pipes, yet their basic understanding had been around the idea of ice, which I had not checked! I may have done three weeks teaching on hard water, but clearly, my students had not learned what I wanted them to learn because I had not used my classroom assessment practices to probe their thinking so that I could help them sort out any problems and connect ideas together.

On joining King's College London, I started my work on a PhD, supervised by Paul Black. I was interested in how science teachers used classroom assessment and the effects this had on how children understood the role of assessment. I was fascinated by how sometimes a smart question or an interesting activity would encourage children to talk and discuss their ideas. Sometimes teachers picked up on student ideas and incorporated these into scientific explanations, while other times teachers would perhaps not acknowledge a student's answer, instead giving their expert explanation of the idea. This led me to look at how teachers conceptualize classroom assessment and how this influences the way that they teach. In exploring these ideas, I introduced an intervention in which students kept a diary of their ideas about their learning for each lesson. Every week I summarized the students' main thinking, the problems or difficulties they were encountering, and what they believed the teacher thought was important in the lesson. I gave this weekly summary to the teacher, and my study explored how the teachers responded to this feedback from their students.

At the same time, Paul Black and Dylan Wiliam were constructing their review of AfL, and as Paul was my supervisor, we frequently discussed how the practices I was witnessing in the classrooms of these teachers matched or contrasted with the many research studies they were exploring for their review. It was an exciting and interesting time and clearly an important contributor to my working life from that day to this.

In 1999, shortly after publication of the review, Paul and Dylan asked me to join them in a study that would examine how teachers might implement the AfL ideas they had identified. Working with two mathematics and two science teachers in each of six schools, we began the first of our many studies that explored how teachers use AfL to drive their practice and influence student learning. Over the twenty years since the review, I have been delighted and privileged to witness and report on the many innovative ways teachers have found to make AfL work in their classrooms. It is one of the few aspects of teaching that can truly transform practice, and more than that, teachers like the approach because it helps them understand how their teaching can help their students learn.

Margaret's Story

Long before Black and Wiliam's 1998 review, I came to assessment for learning through teaching. As a brand-new teacher, I had a class of thirty 7-year-old students, who had recently arrived in the UK from the Punjab in India—they did not speak English, and I did not speak Punjabi, and my job was to teach them.

I quickly realized that if I were going to be in any way effective, I needed to know something about my students, so I made home visits to their families with an interpreter, I went to celebrations at the Sikh temple, and I tried to learn some Punjabi but without a whole lot of success. That first experience of teaching shaped my thinking about assessment; I needed to understand who the students were I was teaching, what they knew, and what was next for them in order to progress day by day. And if they were not progressing day by day, why were they coming to school—and for that matter, why was I?

In the days when I was a classroom teacher, we didn't use the specific terminology that has emerged to describe the practice of AfL, but we did have aims and objectives, and we knew that our job was to figure out how our students were moving forward to meeting those aims and objectives. So I was essentially "wired up" for assessment for learning from my early days in education.

My move to the United States at the end of 1989 coincided with a long period of high-stakes testing for purposes of accountability. Unfortunately, this emphasis narrowed the curriculum and led to distortions in teaching and learning (Hamilton et al., 2007; McMurrer, 2007; Valli & Buese, 2007). Because I have always cared deeply about the quality of teaching and learning and believe that what formally became AfL benefited students, I jumped at the opportunity to become involved in a group of professionals from state departments of education who were concerned with promoting AfL in their respective states. For the past nine years, I have led the group, and we have made great gains in establishing AfL in the US.

About six years ago, I met Christine. We clicked immediately. Our views on teaching and learning and the role of assessment were in synergy, and we liked each other as well! We decided we wanted to write together and cooked up this book project. We are grateful to Corwin for giving us the opportunity.

We have written the book primarily for teachers, but we also think that school and district administrators, policy makers, and students and instructors in teacher preparation and master's degree programs will find much of value in its pages. Each chapter calls on practice-based evidence to both enrich and exemplify understanding of AfL from both research and practice standpoints and so provides a good "sounding board" for teachers and others to explore and reflect on their own practices and beliefs.

Throughout the book, we use vignettes of classroom practice from both countries to illustrate AfL in action.

In Chapter 1, we revisit Black and Wiliam's 1998 ideas to lay out the starting points for AfL in the UK and the US. Chapter 2 provides a rich and nuanced discussion of how the implications, legacy, and opportunities afforded and inhibited by policy and competing priorities affected how teachers in the UK and the US took up AfL and adapted how they worked in classrooms with their students. Chapter 3 traces how expanded conceptions of AfL have embraced existing theories about learning, particularly sociocultural theory, self-regulated learning, and mindsets. In Chapter 4, we focus on AfL in the disciplines and provide practical examples of planning for disciplinary learning and protocols to guide teachers' instructional planning and disciplinary-based AfL. Chapter 5 addresses the transformations teachers make in their classroom practice that allow and enhance the feedback loops between students and teacher and within collaborative learning groups. Our final chapter addresses the unanswered questions in AfL and considers areas for further exploration in research and practice.

We hope you enjoy reading this book as much as we have enjoyed our collaboration in writing it!

REFERENCES

Andersson, C., & Palm, T. (2017). The impact of formative assessment on student achievement: A study of the effects of changes to classroom practice after a comprehensive professional development programme. *Learning and Instruction*, *49*, 92–102.

Andrade, H. L., Bennett, R. E., & Cizek, G. J. (Eds.). (2019). *Handbook of formative assessment in the disciplines.* New York, NY: Routledge.

Bailey, A. L., & Heritage, M. (2018). *Self-regulation in learning: The role of language and formative assessment.* Cambridge, MA: Harvard Education Press.

Black, P., & Wiliam, D. (1998a). Assessment and classroom learning. *Assessment in Education: Principles Policy and Practice, 5*, 7–73.

Black, P., & Wiliam, D. (1998b). *Inside the black box: Raising standards through classroom assessment.* London, UK: Department of Education & Professional Studies, King's College London.

Black, P., & Wiliam, D. (1998c). Inside the black box: Raising standards through classroom assessment. *Phi Delta Kappan, 80*(2), 139–148.

Cowie, B. (2005). Pupil commentary on assessment for learning. *Curriculum Journal, 16*(2), 137–151.

Crooks, T. J. (1988). The impact of classroom evaluation practices on students. *Review of Educational Research, 58,* 438–481.

Hamilton, L. S., Stecher, B. M., Marsh, J. A., McCombs, J. S., Robyn, A., Russell, J. L., . . . Barney, H. (2007). *Standards-based accountability under No Child Left Behind: Experiences of teachers and administrators in three states.* Santa Monica, CA: RAND.

Harrison, C. (2015). Assessment for learning in science classrooms. *Journal of Research in STEM Education, 1*(2), 78–86.

Hattie, J., & Timperley, H. (2007). The power of feedback. *Review of Educational Research, 77*(1), 81–112.

Heritage, M. (2010). *Formative assessment: Making it happen in the classroom.* Thousand Oaks, CA: Corwin.

Kingston, N., & Nash, B. (2011). Formative assessment: A meta-analysis and a call for research. *Educational Measurement: Issues and Practice, 30*(4), 28–37.

McMurrer, J. (2007). *Choices, changes, and challengers: Curriculum and instruction in the NCLB era.* Washington, DC: Center on Education Policy.

Shepard, L. A., Penuel, W. R., & Pellegrino, J. W. (2018). Using learning and motivation theories to coherently link formative assessment, grading practices, and large-scale assessment. *Educational Measurement: Issues and Practice, 37*(1), 21–34.

Valli, L., & Buese, D. (2007). The changing roles of teachers in an era of high-stakes accountability. *American Educational Research Journal, 44*(3), 519–558.

Wiliam, D., Lee, C., Harrison, C., & Black, P. (2004). Teachers developing assessment for learning: Impact on student achievement. *Assessment in Education: Principles, Policy & Practice, 11*(1), 49–65.

Willis, J. (2007). Assessment for learning: Why the theory needs the practice. *International Journal of Pedagogies and Learning, 3*(2), 52–59.

Acknowledgments

This book has its origins in Paul Black and Dylan Wiliam's landmark review on formative assessment, published as *Inside the Black Box* in 1998. Their work paved the way for better teaching and assessment practices, and we are indebted to them for their major contribution to helping all students learn across the world.

Since their review was published, we have both worked with some extraordinary teachers who have shown us what formative assessment can look like in practice. In particular, Margaret offers her gratitude to Gabriela Cardenas, Olivia Lozano, and Mayra Carrasco, whose exemplary classrooms have been a laboratory for her and others to understand the complexities and nuances of formative assessment. Chris would like to thank Paul Spenceley, one of her first project teachers, who has continued to work on and share his teaching ideas; Jason Harding, who was not only an exemplary teacher using these ideas but who has since worked with many teachers on research projects with her; Sally Howard, who helped Chris develop and explore formative assessment in primary classrooms; and Catarina Correia and Natasha Serret for their support in research.

We also thank those teachers who have shared their struggles and challenges with us over the years and who have always been willing to stay the course and find ways to overcome difficulties because they believed that assessment for learning would benefit their students. We have learned a great deal from them, too.

Margaret has a special word of thanks for the members of the Formative Assessment State Collaborative in the United States, who have been steadfast in their commitment to advancing formative assessment across the nation and have contributed so much to the development of her thinking. Chris wishes to thank the Association for Science Education for their continued work in promoting and creating opportunities for teachers, researchers, and educators to work together to strengthen and improve teaching and learning in STEM classrooms

We are most grateful to Jessica Allan from Corwin for her support in publishing this book and for her patience when we were so often behind schedule in our writing!

Finally, Margaret thanks her husband, John, for his unwavering encouragement, and Chris thanks her daughter, Lorenza, for championing these ideas in her own teaching.

About the Authors

Margaret Heritage is an independent consultant in education. For her entire career, her work has spanned both research and practice. In addition to spending many years in her native England as a practitioner, a university lecturer, and as a county inspector of schools, she had an extensive period at University of California, Los Angeles (UCLA), first as principal of the laboratory school of the Graduate School of Education and Information Students and then as an Assistant Director at the National Center for Research on Evaluation, Standards and Student Testing. She has also taught in the departments of education at UCLA and Stanford. Her work is published in peer-reviewed journals, edited books, and practitioner journals. Her most recent book is *Progressing Students' Language Day by Day* (with Alison Bailey), published in 2018 by Corwin.

Christine Harrison is a professor in science education at King's College London, where she works as a researcher and teacher educator. Chris's career began in schools and developed through curriculum development projects and examining in the UK before she began working on her own research. Working at a prestigious university and also spending considerable time in classrooms on research and supporting preservice teachers, Chris realized that there was a gap between research ideas and practice. To that end, she has worked with many teachers, researchers, and organizations, helping all learn from practice-based evidence so they can understand how practice across a variety of contexts centers around the principles of the research. Her work is published in peer-reviewed journals, edited books, and practitioner journals, and she has produced several online courses for teachers and researchers. Chris is Associate Director (London) for the Centre for Innovation in Teacher Education and Development (CITED), which is a joint institutional strategic initiative between Teachers College, Columbia University and King's College London, committed to the principles of equity and social justice. She is also a leading STEM educationalist in Europe working at research, practice, and policy level.

Inside the Black Box Revisited

We noted in the Preface that as an approach to teaching, assessment for learning (AfL) has developed considerably over the last two decades in many parts of the world. In this chapter, we revisit the ideas from Black and Wiliam's review (*Inside the Black Box*, 1998b) that have made such an impact on educators' thinking about teaching, learning, and assessment. Let's begin by defining AfL.

AfL is a range of practices that encourages both teachers and learners to seek evidence of the ways in which students are developing their knowledge, skills, and understanding with the intention of using the evidence to inform learning. AfL requires a dynamic approach to assessing learning with assessment opportunities embedded into the ongoing learning activities and interactions in the classroom. Evidence of learning for both teachers' and students' use is generated from these classroom activities, is explored, and then acted upon during the learning. This process stands in contrast to teachers administering tests, taking students' papers away to grade, or giving feedback at a later date. Assessment used at the point of learning is more likely to reveal what is needed to move forward so that teachers can make judgments about what the evidence shows and act in the immediacy of learning to secure progress for each student.

> *Assessment used at the point of learning is more likely to reveal what is needed to move forward so that teachers can make judgments about what the evidence shows and act in the immediacy of learning to secure progress for each student.*

A New Way of Thinking About Assessment

While the practices that we now identify as AfL have always been within the repertoire of good teachers, the process of actively seeking evidence of learning during classroom activities and intentionally using that evidence to make decisions about next steps has only really come to the fore since Paul Black and Dylan Wiliam's 1998 review. Prior to this, assessment in many schools and classrooms, both in the UK and the US, had generally been thought of as a separate activity from the teaching and learning process, often conceptualized as a quiz, test, or examination coming at the end of a unit of study.

Black and Wiliam's (1998b) review was written at a time when accountability for schools had been high on the agenda of the UK government for the previous decade. This political background had led many schools—and particularly teachers in England and Wales, where a range of legislation and reform had led to a more centralized system with less autonomy for schools—to focus almost exclusively on performance in examinations. Perhaps the most pernicious of the UK government's actions was the introduction of published League Tables that compared examination results across schools. Unsurprisingly, this action resulted in a backwash effect that concentrated teachers', students', and parents' perceptions of classroom assessment as the means to produce scores on achievement tests. Even though some year groups, known as grade levels in the US, were not nationally tested, this more summative approach to assessment was rampant across all years of schooling.

Black and Wiliam's review presented teachers with a new way of thinking about assessment. Rather than the predominant view of assessment as the means to compare and rank students and schools, their review conceptualized assessment as a method of providing qualitative insights, guidance, and feedback during the process of learning. They also helped teachers to recognize that students were actively involved in the process, receiving feedback about their learning and how they could improve from teachers, peers, and from their own internal self-assessment.

Of great significance, Black and Wiliam's review also presented evidence that a more formative approach to assessment raised achievement. Such a goal was desirable to all stakeholders, but for teachers, a formative approach just made sense in terms of helping children learn. This approach to assessment eventually changed the way that classrooms worked by enabling teachers to recognize and respond to learning as it unfolded, rather than simply measuring it at the end of a more or less extended period of learning for summative purposes, and using this measure for grading, reporting, or ranking.

A Systematic Review

Black and Wiliam produced a systematic review, which provides a broader and more detailed analysis of a research field than a meta-analysis (in which only quantitative results are compared). Consequently, systematic reviews generally give a better indication of what actually happened in the classrooms being studied and provide clearer and more informed guidance for teachers and schools on what such practice looks like in action. Black and Wiliam's review consisted of a detailed analysis of some 250 academic articles, book chapters, and books from an initial trawl of 560 publications that focused on assessment during the learning process and which resulted in raised achievement or improved learning behaviors. Some of these publications described quantitative studies where control and experimental classes or groups were compared pre- and postintervention. The majority of the publications in the review, however, focused on more qualitative studies that informed the classroom practices that ultimately resulted in improvement.

Black and Wiliam's extensive systematic review was first published as an academic paper, "Assessment and Classroom Learning," in the journal *Assessment in Education: Principles, Policy and Practice* (1998a). To support and encourage teachers to engage with the ideas in the review, Black and Wiliam also published a twenty-page booklet, *Inside the Black Box* (1998b), which conveyed the key messages from their review. A US version of this booklet was published later that year in *Phi Delta Kappan* (1998c). At the heart of *Inside the Black Box* was the message that learning is driven by the interactions between teachers and students in the classroom. We will return to this powerful idea later in the book.

What Is the Black Box?

The analogy of the *black box* was derived from systems engineering, casting the 1998 UK educational system as focused only on inputs and outputs (and, indeed, the same could be said of the US). Black and Wiliam wanted to explore how the system itself worked. In this analogy, the black box was the classroom and the focus of the review was the teaching and learning that went on inside that box. By investigating what goes on inside the classroom, we can assess whether, how, and in what ways the inputs (teaching, resources, support) truly affect the outcomes we desire for our students.

Because of the more summative approach to assessment that had prevailed in the UK prior to 1998, Black and Wiliam made clear that the form of assessment they were interested in was separate from testing and had a formative purpose. It involved teachers directly collecting evidence of learning and progress from observing learners during activities and reflecting on the conversations and interactions that arose in the classroom.

> By investigating what goes on inside the classroom, we can assess whether, how, and in what ways the inputs (teaching, resources, support) truly affect the outcomes we desire for our students.

Through this approach, Black and Wiliam advanced the idea that assessment can happen naturally as teachers and students go about their classroom activities and that assessment allows teachers to see both what students are learning as well as how they are managing their learning. Students' own self-assessment informs them of how well they are doing in their learning, helps them to recognize what they find easy and what they find difficult, and so provides students with guidance on where they need to focus their effort. Both the teachers' and students' assessment experiences create feedback situations that inform future teaching and learning.

The Assessment Reform Group, a collaboration of assessment experts in the UK, took the message that there was a need for change and a necessity to focus on a more formative approach to assessment as highlighted by the Black and Wiliam review. It was this group that coined the term *assessment for learning* (AfL) as a description of the classroom practices that created a more formative approach to assessment, distinguishing these practices from assessment **of** learning, which referred to examinations, tests, and quizzes that measured performance rather than informed teaching and learning.

Getting Into the Details

AfL entails teachers noting and reflecting on observations of students working individually or in groups, analyzing and assessing artifacts they produce in activities, and listening carefully to the many learning interactions in the lesson. With the evidence they obtain through these means, teachers can recognize and pinpoint areas of partial understanding, which then enable them to respond to and put in place support for the next steps in learning as they arise. By intentionally noticing specific pieces of evidence, teachers are more able to meet the needs of individual learners and respond to these in the activities that follow.

Through taking an iterative approach of collecting evidence and making judgments, the process only becomes *formative* when there is a response either by the teacher, the student, or both that affects future learning. The response might be returning to previous ideas to ensure they are more consolidated before moving on. Often, the response means diverting from the main activity path to ensure students strengthen a particular skill or acquire a piece of knowledge to take their current learning forward. Occasionally, a response requires teachers to put aside the planning they have done and move students on to a more complex activity because the evidence indicates that most students have understood better and more quickly than the teacher had anticipated.

To elaborate further, let's consider how teachers might move from considering evidence to taking action in the classroom. For instance, if the evidence from a foreign language classroom indicates that several students are struggling to locate the appropriate tense to use in their writing in Spanish, the teacher might introduce some activities that focus on strengthening this language aspect before students return to their writing. In another classroom, perhaps the teacher recognizes from the evidence collected that specific students have become very adept at choosing similes and metaphors and so might use these as good examples with the whole class or perhaps pair up these adept students with other students who need some coaching in using or devising similes and metaphors. Perhaps a teacher notices in science investigations that students need practice in recognizing trends in data before moving on to more complex inquiries. Here, the teacher might provide some sets of secondary data within that topic area and model how analyzing the data, using graphs or bar charts, can suggest relationships between particular variables. These relationships could then be tested with students deciding how to control and manipulate the variables in their investigation. In each case, AfL encourages teachers to be responsive to their students' needs; sometimes their response might require consolidation of earlier learning while, at other times, their response might incorporate the strengths identified in learning to move ideas forward.

Three Research Questions

In their review, Black and Wiliam asked three research questions:
1. Is there evidence that improving formative assessment improves standards?
2. Is there evidence that there is room for improvement?
3. Is there evidence about how to improve formative assessment?

Their analysis of the large body of evidence they accumulated concluded that the answer to all three questions was a firm *yes*. What follows is a description of how Black and Wiliam came to their conclusion in relation to each question, which gives us a better understanding of the AfL pedagogy that has developed in the years since the review and which we will discuss more specifically in subsequent chapters.

Is There Evidence That Improving Formative Assessment (AfL) Improves Standards?

To answer this question, Black and Wiliam selected twenty or so quantitative studies that demonstrated significant, and often substantial, learning gains in response to classroom interventions where the ways in which learners received feedback were changed. These studies were from several countries and were wide-ranging in terms of the size of the student cohort, the age of the students, the subjects being taught, and the learning contexts. In every case, control and experimental groups were set up and the improvements between the two groups compared postintervention.

Such a research approach provides evidence on whether an intervention works but provides little or no evidence for understanding how and why new approaches work in classrooms and so does not give much guidance for teachers interested in developing similar interventions in their own classrooms. Fortunately, Black and Wiliam examined over two hundred other research studies that provided some of the detail that teachers need in order to conceptualize what new practice might look like in their context and what changes they may need to make in their own classrooms for themselves as teachers and for their students as learners.

An Example of the Studies Reviewed

One quantitative study that Black and Wiliam reviewed was undertaken by Frederiksen and White (1997) in Chicago in the context of developing an inquiry-based middle school science curriculum. The inquiry was focused on force and motion and involved twelve classes of thirty students each in two schools. All of the classes were organized into peer groups that worked through a sequence of experiments and computer simulations, using an inquiry-cycle model that was made explicit to the students. Each class was divided into two halves: A control group used some periods of time for a general discussion of the module, while an experimental group spent the same amount of time on reflective assessment, which included both self-assessment and peer assessment of presentations students made to the class. The outcome measures were of three types: (1) a mean score on projects throughout the course; (2) a score on two chosen projects, which each student carried out independently; and (3) a score on a conceptual physics test. On all three measures, the experimental groups outperformed the control groups, indicating that time spent on reflective assessment alongside the learning benefited these students.

Common Features Across the Studies

The review found several important common features across the studies. First, all the studies indicated that teachers needed to develop a new approach to pedagogy that enhanced feedback between them and their students. Many teachers think of feedback as a task they do when they comment on or grade student work. The studies reported in the review suggested a different approach to feedback, showing its main purpose was to provide teachers with evidence of how their students were learning so that they could then make a judgment about the degree to which their teaching and choice of activities were helping students learn a particular concept or skill. From the evidence of individual and group learning that teachers elicited during the learning process, they could begin to understand teaching in terms of how they were or how they were not helping students to learn and take action either immediately in the classroom or in planning for subsequent learning experiences.

Second, the studies suggested that more active approaches to learning that engaged and encouraged students to have discussions about what was being learned were more effective. This finding indicated that classrooms in which feedback evidence was generated and used required students to be interactive either directly with their teacher or through working collaboratively with their peers. In the latter case, teachers could then sample group discussions and look at their collaborative endeavor to collect the feedback evidence needed for formative responses.

> Classrooms in which feedback evidence was generated and used required students to be interactive either directly with their teacher or through working collaboratively with their peers.

Third, the studies reported that actions needed to be taken in response to the feedback evidence. In other words, this approach was not about collecting more assessment data but about teachers exploring and reviewing the evidence collected, making decisions about what to do next, and then taking steps that they believed might enhance future learning. Simply put, both decisions and action needed to take place for AfL to occur.

Finally, the studies indicated that teachers needed to be aware of how formative action affected individual students' motivation and self-esteem. While encouraging self-assessment, the review pointed out that making changes in the ways students assess themselves was a complex task and needed careful handling. Interestingly, in those studies in the review where improvements for high-achieving compared to low-achieving students were considered, low-achievers made greater progress than their high-achieving peers. This suggests that while AfL pedagogy helps all students, it particularly supports struggling learners.

Is There Evidence That There Is Room for Improvement?

To answer this question, Black and Wiliam looked to government reports, reports from school inspectors both in the UK and internationally, and research studies. These sources revealed that there were problems and shortcomings in the ways assessment was carried out in some classrooms. Evidence collected from classroom observations, teacher surveys, and teacher interviews indicated that there was room for improvement in assessment practices. The biggest problems at the time were that teachers' tests and quizzes tended to encourage rote learning, many assessments were not shared and discussed within the teaching community, and sometimes the quantity of work or presentation was rewarded instead of the quality. These factors suggested that assessment was not being used effectively and productively in classrooms and was perhaps of relatively low quality.

There were also problems with the ways that teachers collected and recorded assessment data and how they gave feedback to students. Assessments tended to lead to an amalgamation of quantitative data, such as test scores, whereas little was done to analyze student work and performance to discern learning needs. While teachers might provide written or oral feedback on test performance, the feedback often served a social and managerial function rather than a learning function. This meant that advice for improvement was not a general part of the feedback process, and assessments were being used to measure and record achievement rather than promote improvement.

A further concern raised in the literature was that marks and grades were overemphasized when teachers gave feedback to students, which led students and others to focus on their achievement level rather than the learning function of assessment. Within schools and districts, assessment data were used for a large number of purposes, often related to accountability requirements, which could sidestep the learning function of assessment. In such an environment, where the focus was on test scores and grades, feedback to individuals might suggest to some students that they lack "ability," while leading others to believe they are smart and capable. These beliefs, particularly when met at an early age and then continued through schooling, can seriously inhibit children taking an active role in the learning process. High achievers do not want to take challenges as they dare not risk failure, while low achievers shun challenges because they become demotivated and believe they cannot learn. If the focus of classroom assessment is on measurement and comparison rather than guidance for improvement, it creates a classroom atmosphere where students are scared to make mistakes rather than being willing to attempt challenging work, realize that they can learn from their mistakes, and so improve and do a better job next time.

Is There Evidence About How to Improve Formative Assessment (AfL)?

Inside the Black Box noted three areas as likely to improve the effectiveness of classroom assessment: (1) active engagement of students in their own learning; (2) planning to reveal students' thinking; and (3) classroom routines. In fact, the three areas overlap and are clearly interrelated, which is not surprising because they each contribute to the ways in which teachers can support student learning.

Active Engagement of Students. To engage more actively in their learning, students need to understand the process of assessment and what constitutes good learning for particular subjects and age groups. This means that teachers need to help students develop self-assessment skills. To do this, students need a clear vision of what the target of their learning is meant to achieve. They can then consider, with their teacher and peers, where their current learning toward that target stands and discuss how they might begin to "close the gap" (Sadler, 1989, p. 121) between the desired learning and their current learning status. Such understanding by students enables them to focus their efforts on specific aspects of their learning and take an active role in their own improvement.

Planning to Reveal Thinking. While teachers need to plan for learners to be at the center of the classroom assessment process, they also need to select and plan activities where students talk and reveal their thinking. When teachers create opportunities for students to talk, they can recognize evidence about what ideas they have, how they are making connections between ideas, and areas of learning where they are unsure or have gaps in their knowledge and understanding. A key aspect to planning is how the teacher designs and runs these activities in the classroom. If most of the talk is initiated by the teacher and most of the questions asked are directed at simple checking of facts, then this indicates to students that their role is quite passive. In these situations, students are not required to think because questions generally only demand students to recall ideas rather than apply their knowledge to new contexts or analyze ideas from different perspectives. So AfL demands that teachers focus their questions to encourage students to think and challenge their existing ideas.

Classroom Routines. Students quickly learn about their classroom role from the ways in which teachers set up routines and practices. In question-and-answer sessions, if teachers often require an immediate response to their question, most students have insufficient time to work out answers, and the consequence is that only a few students attempt answers or, in some instances, the teacher even answers the question for the students. This type of practice conveys to students that teachers are chasing correct answers, and as a result, classroom talk focuses on students offering answers that fit in with teacher thinking. For classroom talk to be productive

It is essential that discussion evokes thoughtful reflection in which all students are encouraged to take part, with acceptance that ideas need to be shared and explored within the classroom activities.

in a formative way, teachers need a different approach in which they probe and draw out student thinking, as it is the development of student thinking, guided and curbed through feedback and discussion, that results in learning. It is essential that discussion evokes thoughtful reflection in which all students are encouraged to take part, with acceptance that ideas need to be shared and explored within the classroom activities.

Black and Wiliam's review recognizes that tests, quizzes, and homework activities might give the teacher some indication of how students are performing, but it makes clear that they need to be tailored to identify student strengths and needs rather than be used as a measure. Designing and structuring an activity so that it creates evidence of student thinking is not a simple task because it requires the creation of opportunities for thinking, discussion, and consideration of both current and earlier ideas.

Changing Practice

Changes in practice suggested in *Inside the Black Box* are quite demanding for teachers because they are prompted to reflect on what they currently do, which will likely affect how both they and their students work in the classroom. Such reflections begin with thinking about the amount and quality of feedback that teachers are getting from the evidence of students' learning and the possible changes they can make that encourage students to reveal and recognize their needs. Teachers are also prompted to reflect on how they design and adapt activities that encourage thinking and talk so that evidence of learning and feedback drive next steps in learning.

AfL also requires a recognition of the profound influence assessment has on the motivation and self-esteem of students. While it has been widely reported that summative assessment demotivates students (e.g., Harlen & Deakin Crick, 2002, 2003), AfL helps them become more successful learners, which increases their motivation and self-efficacy (Wiliam, 2011). Right from the beginning of implementing AfL, students need to understand that teachers are interested in them as individuals and that teaching is about helping every learner make progress. In such an environment, assessment is not about comparison and ranking students, but rather about providing learners with feedback about the qualities of their work and suggestions for how they can move forward.

Assessment is not about comparison and ranking students, but rather about providing learners with feedback about the qualities of their work and suggestions for how they can move forward.

Putting Ideas From *Inside the Black Box* Into Practice

As we have discussed, Black and Wiliam's review explored AfL from a range of perspectives that included how teachers plan and implement classroom activities, the students' role as active learners, and the ways in which teachers and students respond to feedback. They concluded that there was no direct, simple, optimum model of formative practice; however, their conclusions drew out implications for the policy for and practice of AfL in the classroom.

Guiding Principles
••

Even though no single model on which policy might be based emerges from their review, what does emerge is a set of guiding principles, with the general caveat that the necessary changes in classroom practice are central rather than marginal and that they have to be incorporated by each teacher into his or her practice in his or her own way. In this regard, Black and Wiliam's review stressed that these necessary reforms to practice will inevitably take a long time and require continuing support from both practitioners and researchers. We will return to these ideas later in the book.

Two decades later, we now have examples of Black and Wiliam's ideas in practice and, as predicted, these practices evolved and developed within individual classrooms, though the majority were initially stimulated and shaped through teachers working together to bring about changes that AfL implementation required.

One of the first groups of teachers to start developing the ideas from the Black and Wiliam review participated in an eighteen-month project between 1999 and 2001—the King's–Medway–Oxfordshire Formative Assessment Project (KMOFAP; Black et al., 2003). Initially, KMOFAP researchers worked with twenty-four teachers—two science and two mathematics teachers from six schools. The teachers began with a six-month phase in the latter part of the school year to reflect on how they currently collected evidence of learning in their classrooms and consider what changes they might make in their practice to do this better. The teachers met with the researchers and discussed which ideas might work in their classrooms, what they might need to change to bring these ideas into their practice, and how they anticipated their students would respond to such changes.

Over the next few months, the teachers put some of these ideas into practice. They met every four to six weeks in the teacher/researcher group to discuss progress and problems. Two members of the research team visited the teachers every three weeks, observing lessons in which the teachers were attempting to make changes to their assessment practices and interviewing them afterward about how they thought formative practice was working and how both they and their students were responding to these changes.

The two vignettes that follow are indicative of the types of the early changes the KMOFAP teachers made in their classrooms.

High School Science Lesson

Sarah, a high school science teacher, had decided that she needed to probe student ideas more during her lessons. She planned for this in two ways. First, she thought about the activities that her students were going to do. The scheme of work (syllabus) that had been developed previously by one of her colleagues suggested that the teacher should demonstrate four examples of forces in action and then draw out students' ideas about what forces can do.

Sarah's concern was that possibly only a small number of students would be involved in discussing and thinking about what they observed happening in the three examples being demonstrated. To encourage more students to participate in the classroom dialogue, she decided to set up three sets of the demonstrations around the classroom with brief instructions on the methods for each. Students then did the practical activities in groups of three or four, which ensured that they talked with their peers about what they observed and what they believed was happening.

Second, Sarah planned her role in the classroom events. She devised two sets of questions: One set, the student questions, was intended to make students think and discuss their ideas while they were doing the practical activities, while the other set, the teacher questions, was for Sarah to use as she observed and intervened with groups in the class with the intention of obtaining evidence of their understanding.

Student Questions

- What do you see/feel happening?
- Where was the force acting?
- What does this tell us about forces?

Teacher Questions

- How do you know a force has acted in this activity or demonstration or practical activity?
- What is similar about the way(s) the force is acting in these practicals (practical activities)?
- What is different about the way(s) the force is acting in these practicals?

In the lesson, Sarah quickly introduced the class to the activities, and the students spent about half the lesson time trying them out and discussing what they saw happening. Sarah circulated around the classroom, and after ten minutes of observing and listening in to the student conversations, she began asking groups the questions she had planned. Her intention was to find out if the students had come up with some generalized ideas about what was happening in the practical activities. Sarah then held a whole-class discussion to reflect on what the different groups had noticed in the four activities and to generate their ideas about forces. Interestingly, in this part of the lesson students began to link their observations from the practical activities with ways in which forces were experienced in their everyday lives.

In the final part of the lesson, the students watched a short video on how forces were experienced and used in particular ways on rides in amusement parks. Again, this activity led to a discussion of forces in authentic settings, and it was noticeable how students were beginning to talk about the topic with more confidence and to make connections between the different scenarios they had been presented with. The opportunities that Sarah had set up in this lesson helped students develop a shared understanding about forces and their application in everyday life, engaging more deeply with the underlying knowledge.

In the interview immediately after the lesson, Sarah reported the following:

> I have never known them be so vocal in a class discussion. Mostly it's me and one or two of the brighter ones who answer.

> While in the first bit, I heard a range of terms used such as energy, pressure, push, and so on, their language gradually became more precise as they spoke with one another. Sort of refined in a way. Apart from where they struggled with ideas like with the pulleys.

> It was more effort on my part from a planning perspective, but in the lesson itself, I had much more time to listen in to ideas and get a clearer understanding of what individuals and the whole class know and where we need to take the ideas in future lessons. I think they enjoyed it more, too, which helps.

High School Mathematics Lesson

One of the conclusions that Richard had reached at a teacher/researcher meeting was that the layout of his class did not encourage students to discuss ideas. He decided to change his classroom setup, organizing the tables into eight blocks of two tables rather than having them in rows. Richard had also decided that he would try to get more students involved in whole-class discussion by providing pairs of students with mini whiteboards so they could jot down ideas or answers when requested in the discussions.

Richard's mathematics lessons had followed the routine of a demonstration by him of two or three examples on the board and then the class working independently on exercises that practiced these ideas. Richard also decided to make changes to this routine by breaking this particular lesson into three parts. In the first section of the lesson, Richard explained two examples of solving simultaneous equations, but in the third example, he asked students to come up with ideas of how they might begin to solve the equation in a different way. They jotted their ideas down on their mini whiteboards. Richard then selected three of the students' ideas and worked through all three possibilities with the entire class. Two of the possibilities resulted in solutions, but the third revealed an error partway through. What was interesting in this section of the lesson was how Richard began to portray the working out of the solution as the part he most valued in their learning and also how he stressed the importance of learning from mistakes.

In the second part of the lesson, students worked through exercises but with a slight change to their usual practice. Instead of collecting their work and correcting it, Richard asked the students to check with one another every few questions and discuss those that either had a different way of solving the problem or resulted in a different answer. In the third part of the lesson, Richard asked the students, in pairs, to create three challenging simultaneous equations. These questions were then distributed to other student pairs to work out the solutions.

The changes in routines that Richard instigated placed more reliance on the students to work collaboratively and to check with one another whether they felt they were being successful. This more active role for students helped them engage better with the activities and released Richard to circulate around the classroom and check on the progress different pairs of students were making. It also enabled him to coach two students who he noticed were struggling at the start of the second activity and had started to copy answers from another pair on their table. By the final activity, this pair of students had gained confidence, and while they did struggle a little with the challenging equations set them by their peers, they were motivated to attempt the questions.

In the follow-up interview, Richard reflected on the lesson:

It felt a bit awkward at first, partly because of the room but mainly because they were a bit nervous about helping me solve the equations. They are used to getting lots of practice before they answer in front of their mates, but by that time, several have opted out and decided they can't do them. This way did get them all working, but for me, it felt a bit slow and labored. It was better for them but not for me.

Getting them to check each other's answers was brilliant. They could rectify mistakes on the spot rather than waiting for me to mark and return their work. I shall certainly do more of that.

Interestingly, in the write-your-own-question bit, they learned more from constructing the questions than doing them. . . . They started putting in huge numbers such as 410x and 197y to challenge other pairs and started to realize that you needed to think in a backward fashion as to what multiples the number broke down into, and it was interesting how six, seven, and thirteen times tables became ones they wanted to use. I think I was a bit too keen to intervene and offer suggestions, but I have to admit they probably did more math thinking and talking in this lesson than they have ever done with me previously. The added bonus is that I have also got a set of questions I can use with other classes.

These two vignettes illustrate how teachers can begin the change process toward making their practice more formative. While these teachers were in the very early stages of AfL implementation, we can already see some significant changes in their practice and the impact on students. The teachers planned activities that resulted in students being more actively involved in the learning, which created time and space in the lesson to "listen in" to student dialogue. Such practices alter how classrooms work; routines are reorganized with a learning purpose in mind, affecting how they are understood by both the teacher and the students.

Improvement as a Journey

In classrooms where the focus is on AfL, students come to see improvement in learning as a journey and regard feedback from peers and their teacher as opportunities to consider their current ideas and what might be helpful to use to move toward their goal. When teachers regularly give feedback that does not focus on simply what is correct and incorrect, but rather values how students are articulating their ideas and making connections with both previous understanding and new ideas, students come to understand how to work toward improvement. Through this process, they develop the confidence and capability to move their ideas forward, face challenging tasks, and begin to realize that effort and perseverance are worthwhile.

As AfL becomes embedded into the interactions and activities of the lesson, students realize their role and that of their peers in learning and the role of the teacher in guiding and supporting their progress This evolution of practice, in which teachers alter existing routines or make *space* for new routines, takes time and perseverance; it requires both the teacher and the students to try new ways of working with one another and then reflecting on and selecting those aspects that appear to be productive. This adaptation of practice, when underpinned by principles of effective feedback and learning and shaped by the discipline and context, creates a diversity of AfL practice. Teachers really do make the practice their own, as Black and Wiliam urged them to do.

In the next chapter, we tell the stories of how AfL practice has evolved in both the US and the UK since the publication of *Inside the Black Box* in 1998.

REFERENCES

Black, P., Harrison, C., Lee, C., Marshall, B., & Wiliam, D. (2003). *Assessment for learning: Putting it into practice.* New York, NY: Open University Press.

Black, P., & Wiliam, D. (1998a). Assessment and classroom learning. *Assessment in Education: Principles, Policy and Practice, 5,* 7–73.

Black, P., & Wiliam, D. (1998b). *Inside the black box: Raising standards through classroom assessment.* London, UK: GL Assessment.

Black, P., & Wiliam, D. (1998c). Inside the black box: Raising standards through classroom assessment. *Phi Delta Kappan, 80*(2), 139–148.

Frederickson, J. R., & White, B. J. (1997, March). *Reflective assessment of students' research within an inquiry-based middle school science curriculum.* Paper presented at the Annual Meeting of the American Educational Research Association, Chicago, IL.

Harlen, W., & Deakin Crick, R. (2002). A systematic review of the impact of summative assessment and tests on students' motivation for learning (EPPI–Centre Review, version 1.1*). In *Research evidence in education library* (Issue 1). London, UK: EPPI–Centre, Social Science Research Unit, Institute of Education.

Harlen, W., & Deakin Crick, R. (2003). Testing and motivation for learning. *Assessment in Education: Principles, Policy & Practice, 10*(2), 169–207.

Sadler, D. R. (1989). Formative assessment and the design of instructional strategies. *Instructional Science, 18,* 119–144.

Wiliam, D. (2011). What is assessment for learning? *Studies in Educational Evaluation, 37*(1), 3–14.

A Tale of Two Countries

In this chapter, we describe how the practices of assessment for learning (AfL) have developed in the United Kingdom and the United States since the publication of *Inside the Black Box* (1998). You will see a number of similarities in the stories, including the respective high-stakes testing environments with their associated consequences and the challenges that teachers experience as they make changes in their classroom practice. You will also see differences. The UK central government has committed considerable funding to supporting AfL at various times, whereas no financial support for AfL has been offered by the US federal government, despite allocating vast sums of money to the development of summative tests. In the end, though, you will become aware of how AfL is implemented through the efforts of teachers, one by one. Teachers know what is good for their students and have committed to AfL because they want to do their very best for each one of them.

In the next part of the chapter, we tell the story of how AfL has developed in the UK since the publication of *Inside the Black Box.*

The Tale of the United Kingdom

We begin with a focus on the assessment practices that have dominated in the UK over the years and how AfL implementation has been challenged by them.

Assessment Practices

Inside the Black Box was welcomed by teachers when it was published, and twenty years later most teachers in the UK would claim they know what AfL is and would say they include some aspect of AfL in their daily classroom practice. However, despite the inclusion of AfL in most university teacher preparation courses in the UK, the use of AfL in classrooms varies markedly. AfL practice is still patchy despite a huge investment in time and money (Office for Standards in Education, OFSTED, 2008, 2010; Swaffield, 2009) and is generally better established in primary (elementary) than secondary schools. Some of this variation is to be expected because of the implementation of AfL in different subject disciplines or for different age groups, but other variations relate to simply misunderstanding the formative nature of AfL or using assessment intended for formative purposes for other assessment requirements. Another contributory factor to this variation is the often-seen conflict between teachers' own beliefs and other educational priorities that arise through the changing educational landscape and the expectations of parents, colleagues, and head teachers/principals. For instance, while teachers might believe that children learn best through talk and discussion, their school policy might prioritize student writing, so teachers reduce the lesson time spent on talk to make way for more written work. Over time, many changes at both the national and local levels have either supported or mitigated against AfL developing and establishing itself successfully, resulting in different degrees and emphases of practice across and within schools.

The findings from the *Learning How to Learn* (LHTL) project, a major effort to enhance teaching and learning in schools through innovative practice at the classroom and school level conducted from 2001 to 2005, are instructive about UK teachers' beliefs and AfL practices at that time (James, Black, McCormick, Pedder, & Wiliam, 2006). Survey data revealed that many project teachers reported that they were committed to the ideals of AfL:

- 95 percent responded that they believed it was important or crucial that their students were helped to think about how they learn best;

- 93 percent believed it was important or crucial that teachers helped students to assess their own learning; and

- 83 percent believed it was important or crucial that teachers helped students to plan the next steps in their learning (James, McCormick, Marshall, Pedder, & Carmichael, 2005).

However, in general, many fewer teachers reported actually adopting AfL practices in their classrooms:

- 63 percent reported "often" or "mostly" helping students to think about how they learn best;

- 69 percent reported "often" or "mostly" helping students to assess their own learning; and

- 46 percent reported "often" or "mostly" helping them plan their next steps (James et al., 2005).

While there were likely several factors that led to this difference in beliefs and practice, the LHTL project highlighted two factors, in particular, that seemed to explain these differences for most of the project teachers. First, at that time the national educational climate was dominated by the demands of the curriculum and examinations. The pressure on teachers was to "cover" the course or "teach to the test" rather than take the time to explore students' ideas and understanding. The LHTL project teachers referred to *"pressures of curriculum coverage," "pressures of national testing,"* and *"pressures of a tick-box culture."* Such pressures meant that the tensions and dilemmas teachers faced as a result of coping with external pressures prevented them bringing their practice in line with their own educational values.

The second factor was more fundamental in that it centered on what teachers believed their role was in teaching and learning. Many of the LHTL project teachers believed that their role focused only on teaching the content of the subject discipline rather than helping students to learn the ideas and practices associated with the process of learning itself. Other teachers who saw their role more as a blend of developing content knowledge and learning skills realized that AfL provided a means to help them enculture both within their classroom. Putting AfL into practice required many project teachers to acquire new knowledge about learning, develop new skills, and reassess their roles as teachers. They also had the complex task of applying new theoretical knowledge gained through participating in the project, in real classrooms, where routines, expectations, and ways of working had already been established with students and where numerous constraints and pressures influenced teacher thinking and decision-making. We will return to the challenges teachers experience when implementing AfL in Chapter 5. Now we turn to some of the major policy moves that influenced the uptake of AfL in UK schools.

Major Policy Moves in the UK

Of all the policies within education, assessment seems to be the one that is contentious and newsworthy and yet is often relatively conservative and resistant to change. AfL came to prominence in the UK at a time when the public, formal face of national assessment centered on high-stakes examinations, with an associated commentary focused on standards and comparison. In this context, a challenge for teachers has been to navigate assessment for the purpose of measurement and accountability and assessment for informing and guiding ongoing learning in the classroom. Let us consider how this navigational challenge came about in the UK.

What Preceded *Inside the Black Box?*

To understand why AfL was so welcomed by teachers when ideas were first reported in the 1990s, it is important to know something of the UK culture and history of events that preceded *Inside the Black Box*. The 1960s onward saw great societal changes in the UK, including change within the education system. A major change at that time was the introduction of comprehensive schools across England and Wales. Comprehensive schools are secondary schools funded by the central UK government that correspond broadly to public high schools in the US. Comprehensive schools do not select their students on the basis of academic achievement or aptitude, in contrast to the selective school system that had been in place in England and Wales previously, where admission was restricted on the basis of an entrance examination. The structure of the national assessment system remained as it had always been.

However, in 1984 the UK government's education reforms included a new national qualification—the General Certificate for Secondary Education (GCSE) for 16-year-old students. Part of the GCSE qualification was achieved through coursework over two years prior to the written examination at age 16. Student work and the written examination were assessed against national standards to ensure that the same range of knowledge would be required to attain certain grades throughout the UK, unlike the previous system in which grades were awarded primarily according to statistical rules that measured each candidate's performance relative to the cohort. The existence of five examination boards—resulting historically from regional university entrance examinations across the UK—meant there was a range of examinations for schools to choose from in each subject area, giving them more flexibility in selecting assessments that fit with the courses they were offering. In such a system, teachers and schools had a good deal of autonomy, and assessment was seen very much as a servant to the curriculum.

Within a year of the introduction of the GCSE national assessment system for schools in England, the government decided to introduce a National Curriculum for all school subjects and set up the Task Group on Assessment and Testing (TGAT), led by Professor Paul Black, to examine how this new curriculum might be assessed. The TGAT proposed a national assessment system that would satisfy four general criteria:

1. The assessment results should give direct information about students' achievement in relation to objectives—they should be criterion-referenced.

2. The results should provide a basis for decisions about students' further learning needs—they should be formative.

3. The scales or grades should be capable of comparison across classes and schools if teachers, students, and parents are to share a common language and common standards—so the assessments should be calibrated or moderated.

4. The ways in which criteria and scales are set up and used should relate to expected routes of educational development, giving some continuity to a student's assessment at different ages—the assessments should relate to progression.

The TGAT also recommended that a broad indication of progress was required within national assessment and that this should be checked and reported at ages 7, 11, 14, and 16. Checking of progress at ages 7, 11, and 14 was initially planned as a range of tasks that teachers could select from and use in schools, with the final level at age 16 determined by the recently introduced GCSE examinations.

The National Curriculum assessments were introduced only for the core subjects of English (English language arts), mathematics, and science. The first assessments for 7-year-olds were a range of cross-curricular standardized assessment tasks (SATs) to be administered in the classroom. However, government concern over the complexity of their use meant they were quickly replaced by more test-like tasks, given in each of the three assessed subject areas and no longer cross-curricular in design. The change in the SATs led to the use of more traditional test methods at ages 11 and 14. While the TGAT envisioned an assessment system that was integral to the day-to-day work of classroom teachers, these changes, which occurred within the first two years of the introduction of the National Curriculum, resulted in a very different system, with much of the assessment responsibility being taken out of teachers' hands.

This rapid change in educational reform sent many schools into panic mode as they attempted to navigate the new legislation. Teachers were expected to teach a new curriculum to students aged 5, 7, 11, and 14 (the tested years), while still continuing the old curriculum with other age groups. At the same time, teachers were unsure what the assessments for the new curriculum would look like and what the expectations of the achievement standards would be. Not surprisingly, this situation caught the eye of many university researchers who were interested in exploring what was happening at the classroom level and how they might support this transition of practices.

Assessment Reform Group

In 1989, the British Educational Research Association asked a group of assessment researchers, which became known as the Assessment Reform Group (ARG), to investigate the effects of recent assessment changes in UK schools. The aim of the ARG was to ensure that assessment policy and practice, at all levels of schooling, took account of relevant research evidence; in its early years, it particularly focused on studying the introduction of national testing and assessment in the UK. The ARG's main activity was informing and influencing government policy makers and agencies. The ARG also worked closely with teachers, teacher organizations, and local education authority staff to advance understanding of the roles, purposes, and impacts of assessment. As their work progressed, they focused on how assessment affected learning in schools.

Inside the Black Box

In 1996, the ARG asked Paul Black and Dylan Wiliam to undertake a literature review on the use of assessment that assists learning. As we noted in the Preface, they found decisive evidence that "formative assessment" could improve learning, and they published an academic paper for the assessment research community, the main ideas of which were translated into a booklet for practitioners called *Inside the Black Box*. After the publication of the Black and Wiliam review in 1998, there was great interest into how their ideas might be implemented into classroom practice. Black and Wiliam gained funding to develop a program of work with teachers, the King's–Medway–Oxfordshire formative assessment project (KMOFAP). I (Chris) was asked to join them in both supporting the implementation of formative assessment ideas and researching its effect in classrooms. We conducted an eighteen-month project with science, mathematics, and English (English language arts) teachers in three high schools in Medway, a small town about thirty-five miles from London, and three high schools in the rural county of Oxfordshire. For the first six months, we worked with teachers, helping them try out ideas that would improve feedback to both them and their students. We then spent a whole school year mapping the development of AfL in the thirty-six classrooms and examined its effect on attainment, comparing each class's results against a similar control group that had not been trying out these new ideas. This led to the identification of advice for improving classroom assessment, which we published in a second booklet, *Working Inside the Black Box* in 2002, and later gave a more detailed account in a book, *Assessment for Learning: Putting It Into Practice* (Black et al., 2003).

In light of our work, the ARG produced a leaflet that was sent to all state (public) schools in England. It defined AfL as "the process of seeking and interpreting evidence for use by learners and their teachers to decide where the learners are in their learning, where they need to go and how best to get there" (ARG, 2002, p. 1). The ARG explained that AfL is grounded in ten principles; it

- is part of effective planning;
- focuses on how students learn;
- is central to classroom practice;
- is a key professional skill;
- is sensitive and constructive;
- fosters motivation;
- promotes understanding of goals and criteria;

- helps learners know how to improve;

- develops the capacity for peer and self-assessment; and

- recognizes the full range of achievement of a student (ARG, 2002, p. 2).

Between 2002 and 2004, there was great interest in AfL across the UK. Paul Black, Dylan Wiliam, and I were asked to speak at numerous research and practitioner conferences, and the team provided a huge amount of professional learning for professional organizations, local authorities, and schools. I was an adviser on the *Assessment Is for Learning Project*, a national teacher development project across Scotland. The King's College team, led by Black and Wiliam, started working collaboratively with other research groups, such as Mike Atkin's team at Stanford University in the US and Mary James's team at Cambridge University in the UK. It was an exciting and demanding time; we were able to visit and explore AfL practice more broadly, extending our work to look into primary (elementary) classrooms and across a greater range of subject areas in secondary schools.

There was also growing support for AfL at the national policy level, with advocacy (e.g., Blunkett, 2000; Hargreaves, 2004) and materials developed for use in schools (e.g., Department for Education & Science, 2004; Quality & Curriculum Authority, 2003). Perhaps the strongest expression of the central government's commitment to AfL was the *Assessment for Learning Strategy*, a national rollout of professional learning to all schools in England, and the announcement by the Minister of State for Schools and 14–19 Learners that "*the Government has invested £150 million over the next three years for continuing professional development for teachers in assessment for learning*" (Department for Children, Schools and Families, 2008, p. 1). Admittedly, this figure falls far short of that spent annually on examinations. Nevertheless, it was a substantial sum from a professional learning perspective in the UK.

Effects of Changing Assessment Priorities

Following the publication of *Inside the Black Box* and the dissemination of AfL ideas that followed, there was great excitement in schools as teachers started to engage with more formative practices. At the same time, the government and the inspection systems for schools started to increase the pressure on schools to evaluate and report on their effectiveness, thus creating a more demanding, high-stakes accountability system. In this context, assessment was increasingly required to perform an expanded number of functions, from judging individual students to evaluating schools to monitoring national performance. Requiring assessment to fulfill a myriad of functions had dramatic effects on both summative and formative assessment practices in schools.

The Levels System

While the TGAT report had intended that the levels assessment system would only be for use in statutory national assessments as indicators at ages 7, 11, 14, and 16, over time, levels also came to be used as measures for regular in-school assessment, with the goal of monitoring whether students were on track to achieve expected levels by the end of a particular phase of schooling. This change distorted the purpose of in-school assessment, particularly day-to-day formative assessment, as the focus became much more about which level students had reached. Many teachers began to produce tasks set at different levels in an attempt to provide a means of capturing evidence of students working at particular National Curriculum levels. Whereas AfL sought evidence for future planning and direction, the levels system became a means of monitoring and evidencing progress. In fact, schools were so keen to demonstrate progress that they invented subdivisions in the levels in an attempt to track development more frequently. Over time, this process became the main aim for schools and the "level system" mitigated against AfL, as the main assessment focus was demonstrating progress rather than seeking evidence to inform teaching and learning. This resulted in teachers reporting the final level students had been assigned to without providing any details about the students' knowledge, understanding, and skills.

The system of levels had other unfortunate consequences. It encouraged teachers to focus on a student's current level and targets rather than consider more widely the strengths and weaknesses of a student's capability across the entire curriculum. This led to some subjects being favored in terms of allocating teaching time with the result of constraining the curriculum, particularly in areas such as music and the creative arts. Additionally, value systems were established that focused more on achievement of levels than the quality of work students produced. This change in emphasis about what counts in classroom learning had repercussions on students' motivation and attitude toward learning. Within such a system, students came to think of themselves and their progress in terms of levels. When asked how they were doing, children would say that they were "Level 4" in English (English language arts) or "Level 3" in mathematics, yet they could not describe what this meant in terms of what they could do in class either as an individual learner or part of a group.

Perhaps one of the most striking illustrations of this "levels" view is Diane Reay and Dylan Wiliam's 1999 study, which presents 11-year-old students' perceptions of how assessment contributes to their understanding of themselves as learners, leading up to National Curriculum tests at the end of primary (elementary) phase. Although there was some variation in the students' responses, the majority view was that awarding levels revealed something intrinsic about them as individuals, becoming part of their *identity* and reducing the students' perceptions of their complex selves to single scores. For example, one student, Hannah, was clearly anxious about the upcoming national tests and the level she might achieve. She explained this by claiming that she would "be a nothing" if she did not achieve Level 4 (the maximum), which she felt was expected of her. Hannah was recognized within her school as "an accomplished writer, a gifted dancer and artist and yet none of those skills make her somebody in her own eyes" (Reay & Wiliam, 1999, pp. 345–346).

A further problem was that the established assessment system dominated and skewed lesson planning. Rather than focusing on learning or using formative feedback to inform planning, teachers planned lessons that would allow students to demonstrate the requirements for specific levels. In some situations, this encouraged teachers to design and use only classroom assessments that would report a level outcome. Levels did not lend themselves to assessing the underpinning knowledge and understanding of a concept, and as a result, AfL was not always being used as an integral part of effective teaching; the aim of assessment was to obtain a level rather than probing students' understanding and moving learning forward. Simply put, the assessment and learning focus was on the level the students had reached rather than on how to challenge and support their learning and progress.

The level system also skewed and inhibited communication with parents about their children's learning. Teachers reported to parents the specific level their children had achieved or the progress they were making between levels, rather than describing the meaning of the levels in terms of what students knew and could do in lessons and what support they needed to improve. In effect, many teachers were simply tracking students' progress toward target levels. The drive for progress across levels also led teachers to focus their attention disproportionately on those students who were just below level boundaries.

In the high-stakes UK assessment regime, the system became so conditioned by levels that there was considerable challenge and reluctance from teachers and schools to move away from this system. The *Commission on Assessment Without Levels* (the Commission) was set up by the Department for Education in 2015 to provide advice and support to schools in developing new approaches to their own in-school assessment and to ensure they had information to make informed choices about what might work for their students, staff, and curriculum.

The Commission highlighted some of the difficulties in bringing changes to schools' assessment systems. A key one was the extent to which teachers were subject to conflicting pressures in trying to make appropriate use of assessment as part of classroom teaching on a daily basis, while at the same time collecting assessment data to be used in very high-stakes evaluations of individual and institutional performance. These conflicting purposes often had adverse effects on how teachers implemented the fundamental aims of the curriculum, particularly regarding breadth of content and depth of learning.

However, the Commission recognized that there was a need for change in schools, and their report encouraged such change:

The new national curriculum requires a radical cultural and pedagogical change, from one which has been too dominated by the requirements of the national assessment framework and testing regime to one where the focus needs to be on high-quality, in-depth teaching, supported by in-class formative assessment. Changing the culture of levels is not only the key to implementing the new curriculum, but is the key to raising standards by enriching learning and student motivation and enabling teachers to grow professionally and make better use of their time, knowledge and skills. This is an opportunity the profession cannot afford to miss. (Department for Education, 2015, pp. 3–4)

As of September 2016, the assessment system has been overhauled, and children in England no longer receive their assessment results as a National Curriculum level, but as a judgment on whether or not they have reached the national standard expected for their age (grade level). All state (public) schools at primary (elementary) and secondary level now need to demonstrate that they can report the following:

1. How well their students have learned
2. What progress students are making year-on-year
3. That all students are on track to meet expectations
4. How tailored support programs are being used for individuals who fall behind expectations

Evolution in AfL Practice

Inside the Black Box considered the classroom practices of questioning, feedback, self- and peer assessment. In the following subsections, we consider how these areas have evolved since its publication.

Questioning

In the KMOFAP work, most teachers who engaged in strengthening their AfL practice focused on two areas: increasing "wait time" and the technique "No Hands Up." First, they worked on questioning and talk through improving their skills by increasing wait time—the time taken between asking a question and taking an answer (Rowe, 1976)—and rethinking the types of questions they were asking, either by making questions more open to encourage students to raise a range of ideas or by asking higher-order questions (Bloom, 1956) that encouraged students to apply ideas or evaluate or analyze information. At the same time, many project teachers began to teach their students to take a more active role in discussion by introducing techniques such as "'Think, Pair, Share," in which students would exchange ideas as a pair, both constructing and rehearsing answers, before they shared these with a larger group of students.

Second, they implemented the technique of No Hands Up. Raising their hand to answer a teacher's question had been commonplace for students in classrooms before AfL ideas started to develop. However, early during the project two mathematics teachers decided that this practice mitigated against many students taking an active role during class discussions, with some children tending to sit back and let others, possibly more confident students, answer questions in class. By stopping students from putting up their hands to answer, these two teachers reasoned that more children would be encouraged to work out answers, just in case the teacher picked them to respond. Within a couple of lessons of trying this new technique, the teachers brought about quite a change in the way students responded to class questions. Not only were more students engaged and more student ideas were offered, but students also began to admit when they were unsure about an idea or tentative about an answer. This feedback was valuable for the teachers, as they were then able to explore partial understanding and uncertainty and begin to plan how they might move ideas forward. It was also useful for students because they came to a better understanding of their ideas and a realization that the teacher wanted to help them improve. It moved the classroom practice from students guessing the answer to the teacher's question to teachers probing student thinking, while at the same time engaging students more actively in their learning and their self-assessment.

Feedback

An AfL practice that has become more dominant than those initially emerging in classrooms following the publication of *Inside the Black Box* is "comment-only marking," which is when teachers give written or oral feedback on student work and performance about what they have done well and areas they need to improve on. By withholding a final mark or grade until work or a performance has been revised and improved, the student can focus on improvement, and the teacher can give detailed specific targets rather than a comparative judgment.

By withholding a final mark or grade until work or a performance has been revised and improved, the student can focus on improvement, and the teacher can give detailed specific targets rather than a comparative judgment.

For example, a geography classroom of 15-year-olds began the lesson by working in pairs, first reading the feedback that their teacher had written on a homework task about where to re-site recycling collection bins in their town center.

The following is a sample of the feedback notes that the teacher had written for the students.

> **Feedback sample 1:** *You have clearly evaluated how the public can access the site and how it can be made to blend in with the surroundings. Think a bit more about the likely quantity of recycling for a town of this size and capacity on site.*
>
> **Feedback sample 2:** *Good idea to signpost routes to the site. Which factors may limit the size of the site and how will overuse be dealt with?*
>
> **Feedback sample 3:** *Clear representation of the site and thoughts about capacity. How are you going to persuade nearby shops that this is the best site?*

The pairs of students discussed what they thought the teacher feedback was communicating, read one another's work, and also agreed on ways in which each individual might improve his or her own recycling report. On a few occasions, some pairs called the teacher over to either ask for clarification or check that their decisions about improvement were on the right track. The teacher circulated while they were discussing the feedback, listening in on conversations but generally allowing them to sort out their ideas for themselves. The students were then given twenty minutes in the lesson to make the necessary improvements to their work. Students proceeded to add or change ideas in their reports, having been guided by the teacher feedback and peer discussion on specific improvements to their reports.

In this vignette of practice, AfL was championed through careful, differentiated written feedback by the teacher. By noting and recognizing specific improvements in their own report and that of a peer, students were able to take action in the lesson. The circle of formative practice was initiated, and they were able to "close the gap," the discrepancy between their current learning status and the desired goal (Sadler, 1989).

After the lesson, the teacher commented on how effective she felt the AfL strategy was:

> *This helps them see, understand, and do the quality of work I am expecting from them. Last lesson, we watched a video clip of a town planner explaining what he looks for and problems he has had when he changes infrastructure in small towns. They had all begun by thinking the collection site should be outside the town, but that video reshaped how they thought about the use and the dynamics of using a recycling site. This essay assessed whether they could put those ideas together to make it feasible but also acceptable to all parties. I knew they would focus on some bits and miss others. So it was worth the time giving individual comment-only feedback and time to redraft the final work.*

Another popular strategy in recent years has been students directly responding to teacher feedback. Students either write their reaction to any feedback that a teacher has written in a speech bubble on their work, or they write a comment under the teacher's comment. For example, an 8-year-old's teacher provided this written feedback on her review of a poem: "You have explained what the poem is about well, but what do you really like about it?" The student responded in writing, "I liked when the wind blew and blew and the sea gurgled anew. It made me think the sea was alive and could gobble them up." This student had clearly gone back to the poem and done more thinking about it. As a result, she was able to give a more detailed, personal, and focused critique of the poem. What was particularly encouraging about the way the strategy was working here was a further comment of "*Me, too*" from the teacher. In this short exchange of feedback, the learning was continuing through the written discussion, and the student was gradually gaining an idea of what the teacher valued within a review.

While the previous example was successful, there are occasions when this feedback strategy can misfire. Here are some examples of such misfires: In a mathematics lesson for 12-year-olds, a teacher had written, "*Try using your number line to check what happens with -/+.*" The student had written, "Thanks. Will do." Yet in the next piece of work, the student was making the same mistakes in his calculations. So clearly, the strategy was not encouraging improvement.

In a 14-year-old's science notebook, a teacher had written about a neutralization practical, "*Explain why you used excess CuO and why it was important to only gently heat the final product.*" The student had replied, "It said to use excess in the instructions, and we used gentle heating for health and safety because we were heating an acid." Despite this feedback and response being made three weeks prior, there had been no further feedback from the teacher. In fact, on both points this student had the wrong idea. The chemical was used in excess to make sure all of the acid had reacted. By the time the final gentle heating was done, there was no acid. The student would have been heating a copper sulfate solution gently to remove the water, while still allowing the crystals to form. If the teacher had gone back and checked what the student had written, he would have been able to respond to errors the student was still making and to check with others in the class that they had fully understood the practical activity. Sorting out these misconceptions as they arise may deter them from arising again in future activities and would show the student that the teacher is there to help reshape their ideas, rather than just set tasks.

Just as with the earlier vignettes, what is important with all of these examples of practice is that AfL works as a series of pedagogic decisions that are planned for and act as a response to drive learning forward. It is when teachers try to add them on to current classroom routines and procedures that sometimes their purpose gets diminished or lost.

As more of AfL practices begin to focus on judgments of students' work by the teacher outside the classroom with follow-up work next lesson by students, the driving agent behind AfL can get lost. AfL needs to be embedded in classroom practice and decisions made on the evidence that arises during learning. So while "comment-only" marking and activating learners to respond to feedback can work in some situations, there is a possibility that these actions downplay the evidence-gathering process that happens during lessons. This disjuncture could mean that important pieces of evidence arising in lessons that might have helped learners are missed or overlooked.

> *AfL works as a series of pedagogic decisions that are planned for and act as a response to drive learning forward. It is when teachers try to add them on to current classroom routines and procedures that sometimes their purpose gets diminished or lost.*

Self- and Peer Assessment

Since the publication of *Inside the Black Box*, teachers have been keen to develop self- and peer assessment activities. However, one of the problems teachers often encountered was that students did not have sufficient skills to engage fully with self- and peer assessment activities and so such attempts were done superficially. Self-assessment requires students to recognize, validate, and evaluate criteria applied to their work. What many teachers found over time was that development of such skills only occurred if teachers first modeled both the process of self-assessment in the ways that they made judgments of student work and the manner in which they constructed feedback. When teachers started to provide more detailed comments on student work in a language that encouraged improvement, students began to understand how they might be able to provide feedback on their peers' work or how they might reflect on their own work.

In addition, to help with this development of a feedback language, some UK teachers developed tactics such as "Two Stars and a Wish." *Two stars* referred to two strengths in the work, and the *wish* referred to an aspect of the work that might be improved. For example, on a foreign language piece of writing, a student's peer feedback was the following:

- *Good choice of vocabulary.*

- *Adjectives agreed with nouns.*

- *Now check on use of perfect tense with some of your verbs.*

The student has provided two strengths (stars) and a target (wish)—check on the use of the perfect tense.

A second strategy that began with teacher feedback and then was taken on in peer assessment was "Even Better If." Here, the assessor (either the teacher or the peer) would write a general feedback summary of what was achieved and a closing statement that began with "*Even better if . . .*" The following examples give a flavor of how feedback was used by a teacher and a peer:

- *Rich and powerful language with a good outline of the character. Even better if you had given some quotes showing how he interacts with other characters.* (English teacher feedback)

- *Liked the way you explained about the hermit's daily routine. Even better if you gave some ideas about how he might react to the villagers starting to build new forest paths.* (Peer feedback in an English lesson)

- *Rock cycle is well explained. Even better if you had added a diagram to sum up the various processes.* (Geography teacher feedback)

- *Accurate and neat map. Even better if you had put in a title.* (Peer feedback in a geography lesson)

UK teachers have focused on the areas identified as key to AfL in *Inside the Black Box* with a considerable degree of success. However, there have been a number of obstacles along the way to fully and effectively implementing AfL in UK schools.

Obstacles to Implementation

While many AfL practices helped build student confidence in their understanding or performance, there were concerns over the efficacy of some of these practices in promoting feedback and improvement. Teachers frequently report that they "do AfL," and yet, when asked how it was helping learning, many teachers were unable to articulate how. Perhaps they lacked the assessment literacy to explain how AfL prompted the learning process, or they may have simply enacted AfL routines without careful thought about how they were affecting student learning.

Evidence of teachers' lack of AfL understanding came from an inspectorate report (Office for Standards in Education, 2008) that indicated that twenty-seven schools out of a sample of forty-three demonstrated that AfL was having low impact because the teachers in these schools had not understood how the approaches were supposed to improve students' achievement. In particular, the teachers used key aspects of AfL, such as identifying and explaining objectives, questioning, reviewing students' progress, and providing feedback without sufficient precision and skill to modify learning. As a result, students did not understand enough about what they needed to do to improve and how they could achieve their learning targets.

Teachers did not assess learning effectively during lessons, and opportunities for students to assess their own work or that of their peers were infrequent and not always effective. In the sixteen schools designated "good" or "outstanding," AfL was better established in English (English language arts) and mathematics than more widely across the curriculum for both primary (elementary) and secondary schools. Opportunities for students to assess their own work was a key feature of the most successful lessons.

One aspect of AfL that teachers have grappled with over the last twenty years is curriculum coverage and pace. In secondary (high) schools, many discipline areas organize the year's teaching into blocks of topics with a certain time frame allocated to each topic. Allocating specific time periods for topic coverage can be tricky because teachers may need to sometimes slow the pace and sort out problems, while at other times teachers might realize that everyone has a better understanding than she or he had anticipated and so needs to take the decision to ditch or restructure the follow-up activities initially planned. This shaping of next steps in response to evidence obtained during lessons determines the pace of teaching and learning. Sometimes learning will be slow and incremental, while at other times it can take a leap forward. In recent years, teachers adjusting what they do next in response to evidence of student learning or needs has come to be known as responsive teaching (Harrison, 2015), which has two main components. First, the focus of responsive teaching is on moving learning forward, which entails the teacher ensuring that there is sufficient evidence to make a decision about next steps, and then taking the necessary pedagogical action. Second, teachers need to be aware of both the immediate needs of their students and those they were aware of previously and use both these aspects to shape the classroom decisions that they take.

> Teachers need to be aware of both the immediate needs of their students and those they were aware of previously and use both these aspects to shape the classroom decisions that they take.

In the next part of the chapter, we turn to our second tale and trace some of the major landmarks and influences on the practice of AfL in US classrooms since the publication of *Inside the Black Box*.

A Tale From the US

Just Good Teaching?

Some would say that US teachers have always done assessment for learning because, after all, "Isn't it just good teaching?" While effective teachers have attended to evidence of learning and adjusted their teaching accordingly, it would be fair to say that in the 20th century most US teachers had not heard of AfL as a domain of practice, and they did not implement it fully in the way that *Inside the Black Box* envisioned. For instance, while teachers might have used assessments formatively in that they made decisions about student learning from assessment results, most teachers' assessment practice generally did not include explicitly asking questions during a lesson to gain insights into student thinking, providing feedback to students to move learning forward, and supporting students in developing self- and peer assessment skills. Furthermore, much of teachers' teaching and corresponding student learning was inimical to AfL. As a publication from the National Council of Teachers of Mathematics (NCTM) observed, the prevailing paradigm in US classrooms for many years has been review, demonstration, and practice (NCTM, 2014). This approach can be considered a fixed sequence of tasks, focused on correctness and accuracy, which prescribe the learning. Such an approach leads to assessment as a set of procedures and reinforces the notion that the purpose of assessment is to determine if students "got it or didn't get it" (Otero, 2006). In this situation, the primary pedagogical response to assessment information is remediation with little to no room for student involvement in either learning or assessment. Similar charges can be leveled at other subject areas as well. So for many years, AfL, as conceptualized by *Inside the Black Box*, has encountered some very strong headwinds.

However, several developments in the US have occurred since *Inside the Black Box* was published, which have led to both ebbs and flows in the implementation of AfL.

Developments in the US

Assessment expert Rick Stiggins is considered one of the early pioneers of AfL in the US. Since the 1990s, Stiggins has advocated that assessment should assist teachers in understanding and responding to students' learning needs. Furthermore, long before most educators thought that students should be part of the assessment process, Stiggins placed students firmly as active participants in their own self-assessment. Few would dispute Stiggins's influence on practice in the US through his publications and professional learning institutes. However, the US is a very big country, and one person alone cannot change the practice of every teacher. Other individuals and organizations have also impacted the development of the AfL in the US since the publication of *Inside the Black Box*.

Arguably, one of the major landmarks in the US for AfL was the address that distinguished assessment expert Lorrie Shepard made to the American Educational Research Association (AERA) as its president in 2000. In this address, Shepard focused on the "kind of assessment that can be used to support and enhance learning" (Shepard, 2000, p. 4). She explicitly linked the features of AfL—the causal mechanisms—and learning theory to explain how this kind of assessment works, and she concomitantly called for a transformation of assessment practices in US classrooms. Shepard's hope for a shift in classroom practice was a reaction to the dominance of the "culture of testing" in the US, in which, for most of the 20th century, attention to assessment had been focused on large-scale standardized testing (McMillan, 2013). She proposed that the role of assessment should be to promote a "culture of learning" instead of contributing to the prevailing "culture of testing."

Around the time of Shepard's address, two committees of the National Research Council (NRC) produced a report, *How People Learn: Brain, Mind, Experience, and School* (NRC, 2000), that summarized developments in learning research and conceptualizing learning as a matter of meaning making and active knowledge construction on the part of the learner. The committees advocated that this conceptualization needed to replace the idea of the learner as an empty vessel to be filled with knowledge provided by the teacher. In terms of classroom practice, the report noted that the implications of this research are that (1) teachers must work with their students' preexisting understanding; (2) superficial coverage of all topics in a subject area should be replaced with in-depth coverage of fewer topics that allow for key concepts in a discipline to be understood; and (3) teachers need to teach metacognitive skills as a means to assist students to learn independently.

The report also included a consideration of assessment and stressed the importance of formative assessment and feedback to learning, noting that effective teachers "continually attempt to learn about their students' thinking and understanding" and they also "help students build skills of self-assessment" (NRC, 2000, p. 140). In other words, effective teachers implement AfL.

Not long after *How People Learn* was published, another NRC committee produced what is now regarded in assessment circles as a seminal report, *Knowing What Students Know* (*KWSK*; NRC, 2001). Just as advances in cognitive sciences shed light on the ways that people learn, *KWSK* showed that cognitive science also strongly implies that assessment practices need to move beyond discrete bits and pieces of knowledge to encompass the more complex aspects of student learning, including how their knowledge is organized and whether students can explain what they know (Pellegrino, 2003). *KWSK* proposed an ambitious vision for balanced systems of assessment that examined the broad range of competencies and forms of student understanding that cognitive science shows are important aspects of student learning. *KWSK* referenced Black and Wiliam's 1998 review and specifically called out the importance of feedback to students and the development of their self-assessment skills. Since *KWSK* appeared, many state education agencies (SEAs) across the US have established balanced assessment systems that typically include formative, interim/benchmark, and end-of-year accountability assessments. While formative assessment is sometimes treated as more frequent testing in such systems, many SEAs are clear that it is a set of assessment practices that inform ongoing teaching and learning.

As a result of these important scholarly efforts, new conceptions of learning and teaching and assessment were squarely placed in the US education landscape: AfL practices are consistent with contemporary learning theory; learners are active in constructing knowledge; students need to learn key concepts deeply; assessment should support and enhance learning through teachers paying attention to student thinking while it is in development (as opposed to just measuring it); feedback to students that helps them advance their own learning is a key practice; students need to be taught metacognitive skills such as self-assessment. If all of these conditions were in place, then Shepard's call for a culture of learning rather than one of testing was eminently possible. However, since Shepard's address, the voyage of assessment for learning into US schools has not all been plain sailing.

Obstacles to Implementation

Shepard's AERA address and the two NRC reports coincided with federal legislation, the No Child Left Behind Act (NCLB) of 2001 (GovTrack.us, 2019a), which introduced high-stakes accountability requirements with a menu of sanctions for low-performing schools. NCLB added to the already predominant culture of testing that Shepard had identified by placing increased pressure on teachers and administrators to raise scores on end-of-year standardized tests. While the aspirations of NCLB to close persistent achievement gaps among US students were laudable, some of its collateral effects were not. One might have imagined that because *Inside the Black Box* had shown that AfL could improve achievement, teachers would have an imperative for implementing this type of assessment, but alas, this was not the case. Instead, the implementation of NCLB resulted in a distortion of the curriculum to focus on the tested subjects (English language arts and mathematics) and on the practice of "teaching to the test."

At the same time, test publishers saw an opportunity for commercial sales and rushed to develop formative assessment products. Their logic was that if formative assessment improved achievement, then they would be helping teachers to raise test scores for NCLB through the use of their products. In fact, test publishers misappropriated the formative assessment label (Shepard, 2005); the assessments they developed would be more accurately described as interim or benchmark assessments, administered periodically to monitor student progress toward the standards they were expected to achieve (Perie, Marion, & Gong, 2009). As Dylan Wiliam observed, these assessments were better thought of as "early warning summative assessments" (cited in Shepard, 2005). However, school districts, anxious to raise achievement, purchased many of these interim assessments and considered their implementation as AfL practices. So in line with the predominant testing culture, AfL was treated by test publishers and their many users as a particular kind of measurement instrument rather than a process that is fundamental and indigenous to the practice of teaching and learning.

Unlike the UK, there has been little to no support for assessment for learning at the federal level (i.e., the US government). The most recent authorization of the Elementary and Secondary School Act (formerly known as NCLB and now the Every Student Succeeds Act [ESSA] of 2015), does not serve to clarify AfL (or "formative assessment," as it is referred to in ESSA). Indeed, ESSA perpetuates the misconception of formative assessment as a measurement instrument. For example, among the references to formative assessment in ESSA are balanced assessment systems that include summative, interim, and formative assessments (note the plural s signaling formative assessment as an instrument), support for local educational agencies in developing or improving such assessments, and for principals and teachers in selecting "formative assessments" (GovTrack.us, 2019b).

Impetus for Implementation

Despite the persistent misunderstanding of AfL in many quarters in the US that has been fueled by, among others, federal legislation and commercial test publishers, two recent efforts have provided more fertile ground for its implementation: (1) the introduction of college and career readiness standards (CCRS) in English language arts (ELA) and mathematics along with the introduction of Next Generation Science Standards (NGSS); and (2) a consortium of states focused on supporting the implementation of AfL across their respective states.

Primarily a response to ongoing globalization, the CCRS and NGSS describe the competencies US students need to have when they graduate from high school in order to be productive citizens and effective contributors to economic vitality. To a great extent, the CCRS[1] and the NGSS reflect the recommendations of *How People Learn*, for example, that "fundamental understanding about subjects, including how to frame and ask meaningful questions about various subject areas, contributes to individuals' more basic understanding of principles of learning that can assist them in becoming self-sustaining, lifelong learners" (NRC, 2000, p. 5).

For the most part, the CCRS and NGSS call for more rigorous and ambitious goals for learning, emphasizing deeper learning and meaning making, as well as the inclusion of student dialogue as a significant

---

[1] Originally developed as Common Core State Standards [National Governors Association Center for Best Practices, Council of Chief State School Officers. (2010). Common Core State Standards. Washington, DC: Author], most states have now made amendments to the Common Core Standards to tailor them to states' requirements, hence college and career ready standards, although they are still generally in line with the Common Core.

component in achieving the standards. For example, in mathematics, students are expected to communicate reasoning about concepts, construct viable arguments, and critique the reasoning of others; in science, they must engage in argument from evidence and construct explanations; and ELA standards require students to engage with complex texts to build knowledge across the curriculum and in writing use evidence to inform, argue, and analyze. When students are engaged in dialogue, communicating their reasoning or constructing viable arguments, AfL opportunities that teachers can take advantage of are already built into the lesson.

> When students are engaged in dialogue, communicating their reasoning or constructing viable arguments, AfL opportunities that teachers can take advantage of are already built into the lesson.

In her AERA presidential address, Shepard (2000) spoke about assessment in a learning culture in an effort to get at the "underlying fabric, linking meanings and classroom interaction patterns that have created a 'testing' culture and think instead about the profound shifts that would need to occur to establish a learning culture" (Shepard, 2013, p. xix). Implementing the CCRS and NGSS has required many teachers to change how they think about teaching and learning in their classrooms. In the same vein, the authors of *How People Learn* noted that a challenge of implementing good assessment practices involves the need to change many teachers' ideas of what effective learning looks like (NRC, 2000). Moreover, as we noted in Chapter 1, *Inside the Black Box* envisioned that implementing AfL would require significant changes in classroom practice. The CCRS and the NGSS have required many teachers to change how they do business in their classroom, moving from the teacher doing all the talking and telling students what they should know to engaging students in disciplinary learning that requires inquiry, discussion, and deep thinking. Consequently, they have laid a foundation for the profound shifts that Shepard hoped for. By way of illustration of the kind of changes US teachers are making in their classroom, here is one fourth-grade teacher's reflection:

> I am learning how to teach in a new way. In the past, I did a lot more presentation-style teaching where I talked a lot more and did a lot more of the intellectual work in the classroom. But now I am learning how to hand the reins over to the students so that they are the ones doing the intellectual work—they're the ones doing the heavy lifting.
>
> So I've seen a lot of great things in my classroom, but it is a little bit outside my comfort zone in a productive struggle, positive kind of way to help kids learn this way and for me to learn to teach this way.

When this teacher focuses more on the learning rather than the teaching, she can readily incorporate assessment for learning into her daily classroom practice, which, in fact, is exactly what she has done!

Another significant development in the US was the formation in 2006 of a consortium of states, Formative Assessment State Collaborative (FAST SCASS), established to promote assessment for learning in their jurisdictions. FAST operates under the aegis of the Council of Chief State School Officers (CCSSO), a nationwide membership organization for state education leaders. The FAST group has been instrumental is raising the profile of AfL across the US and has produced a number of resources intended to support AfL in member states and nationwide. In addition, several member states—for example, Oregon and Maryland—have provided funding to develop online courses about AfL with opportunities for teachers to implement AfL ideas with support from a local professional learning community. Other SEAs, such as Michigan and Arizona, have funded and supported sustained professional learning opportunities for teachers in their states to incorporate AfL in their classrooms.

The interest in AfL that has emerged since *Inside the Black Box* is also reflected in a number of professional standards documents: the Interstate Teacher Assessment and Support Consortium Model Core Teaching Standards (InTASC) developed in 2011 by CCSSO require teachers to "understand the difference between formative and summative application of assessment and know how and when to use each (p. 15); the National Board for Professional Teaching Standards (2010) specify that teachers should view ongoing assessment as an integral part of their instruction, benefiting both the teacher and the student; identify and make explicit the learning goals for each lesson; skillfully incorporate opportunities for assessing students' progress into daily instruction; provide timely and constructive feedback; and help students develop the ability to self-monitor and evaluate personal progress.

It may be said that, from shaky beginnings in the US, the practice of AfL is taking hold, and as a result of the introduction of the CCRS and NGSS and professional learning opportunities such as those provided by members of the FAST group, practices are changing. In what ways? To answer the question, we'll now think about changes in the US in relation to the areas that *Inside the Black Box* specifically addressed and that were discussed in the UK section in relation to AfL practice there: questioning, feedback, and self- and peer assessment.

Changes in Practice

Questioning

As noted earlier, classroom dialogue is a central component of both the CCRS and the NGSS. The inclusion of classroom productive dialogue as a means to learning contrasts with the ubiquitous quiet classrooms where students listen to the teacher and then engage in independent practice to consolidate what has been taught. The aim of classroom dialogue is to promote active participation of all members of the class in exploring and thereby developing their understanding of important concepts in discussion with the teacher and with each other. In this context, teachers' questioning practices are instrumental in provoking a rich discussion and then to steering the discussion in productive ways (Black, Wilson, & Yao, 2011).

Let us consider two examples of teacher questioning and their impact on student learning. In the first, taken from Heritage and Heritage (2013), a sixth-grade class has read a poem by Ralph Hodgson (1920) titled "Time, You Old Gypsyman" and, in an effort to get the class to recognize that the true topic of the poem is time, the teacher begins the class discussion of the poem by asking, *"Now then, has anyone anything to say? What d'you think this poem's all about?"* One student offers the idea that "they want the gypsyman to stay one more day," to which the teacher responds, *"Any other ideas? She's not right. That's the answer I expected, but it's not right."* The teacher encourages the students' responses by saying, *"Don't be frightened, don't be frightened, this is not an easy poem."* Students continue to offer ideas, and the teacher's responses include, *"You say we are talking about a gypsyman . . . well, we're not. We are not talking about a gypsy living in a caravan,"* and *"No, it is not about a bird that flies around."* The teacher consistently asks "known answer" questions whose objective is to discover what the student knows (correctly) rather than to engage in a process of reasoning or discovery about the poem. Furthermore, the teacher's questions do not provide opportunities for him to gain insights into student thinking as an AfL strategy, so he moves through the prescribed lesson without reference to students' ideas (Heritage & Heritage, 2013).

In the second example, a teacher began her second-grade mathematics lesson with a class warm-up discussion about grouping eight beads of two different colors to make patterns for a necklace. Here is an excerpt from the discussion:

Student 1:	*Well, that's two and then . . . well, you have to add them up all together because eight is an equal number and so you can do . . . but you can do this with a lot of numbers, but one thing it has is where maybe you have two groups and you can't do that with a seven because all the groups want the same amount. So you can't give three to one group and four to the other group cuz that wouldn't be fair. So you add . . . so it would have to add up to be four and four.*
Teacher:	*So (student 1's name) is saying that the number eight is an equal number. And that it's an equal number whereas seven is not. Hmmm. (Student 2's name), what do you think?*
Student 2:	*Of course, because, say you would count by twos like that, because you see it's an equal number, because four plus four is eight.*

(Continued)

(Continiued)

Teacher: *OK.*

Student 2: *And just like (student 1's name) said, seven is made with three and four.*

Teacher: *So you're saying, (student 2's name), you agree where eight is an equal number.*

Student 2: *Yes.*

Teacher: *Equal in the sense that if we take that number and partition it into two groups we can end up with four and four?*

Student 2: *Yes. And these are the equal numbers, like if I counted by twos. Two, four, six, eight. Those are all equal numbers.*

Teacher: *All equal numbers? Does everyone agree?*

Student 3: *I'm in disagreement.*

Teacher: *What is your disagreement?*

Student 3: *I think every number is an even number because if you take a five, for example, you can split it into two and two, but then you take the extra one and you split it in half.*

After Student 3 had made this proposition, the teacher continued with questions that led students through a discussion of fractions and then to whole numbers, which concluded with the students' agreement on a definition of an even number advanced by one of their peers: "a number made up of two of the same whole numbers."

This teacher was able to listen to student responses, interpret them, and to steer the discussion with a light touch by summarizing and asking further questions (Black et al., 2011). In addition to helping students construct their own understanding, the discussion provided insights for the teacher into how students were thinking about even numbers and eventually whole numbers and fractions (not included in the transcript). She was able to probe these understandings further with individual students while they were engaged in problem-solving, returning to the topic during a plenary session at the end of the lesson so that students could provide feedback to one another about their problem-solving strategies.

Of course, being able to conduct a discussion in the way that the second-grade teacher did requires considerable knowledge and skills, including knowledge of the subject matter and about how students learn that subject, interpretive listening skills, questioning skills, and the ability to steer the discussion in productive directions. As noted earlier, the introduction of the CCRS and the NGSS provided an impetus for teachers to develop and hone their skills that align with the questioning and interpretive skills needed for AfL. The changes for many teachers have been profound, illustrated by the teacher who said,

> I used to think formative assessment was giving more quizzes mid unit. Now I think formative assessment is good dialogue and thoughtful questioning and flexible guidance throughout a lesson to ensure every student is on track.

Feedback

For feedback to be formative, it needs to assist learners in taking action to close the gap (Sadler, 1989). While *Inside the Black Box* made clear that feedback is a key element in AfL, the provision of feedback is among the least well developed aspects of US teachers' practice. Two main reasons account for this situation. First, simply put, the US is a grade-obsessed society. Teachers are required to give grades very frequently for a whole host of social reasons, including *"Students won't do the work without grades," "They motivate students," "Parents want them,"* and *"Administrators say I have to give them."* Giving students grades is not formative feedback. As we know, for feedback to be formative it must be provided while students are in the process of learning. In contrast, grades provide a summative judgment, an evaluation of the learning that has been achieved, and they also do not support the development of self-assessment (Andrade & Heritage, 2017). Because teachers are overwhelmed by the demands of grading, they are often reluctant to consider feedback as an essential part of learning and teaching.

Second, unless teachers adopt the view that learning is active knowledge construction rather than passive information acquisition, they are unlikely to view feedback as important to learning. In this regard, when teachers prescribe learning (e.g., review, demonstration, and practice) and plan sequences of activities within lessons that emphasize correctness and accuracy, there is little room for formative feedback. However, in lessons where the tasks are not imposed on learning but rather can be adjusted in response to student thinking once they have been initiated (Perrenoud, 1998), feedback makes sense—there is scope for students to make their own adjustments while they are in the process of learning, with the guidance of teacher feedback.

Despite the challenges associated with the dominance of grading, many teachers have made the necessary changes in how they think about and use feedback. These changes are well summed up by one teacher who observed the following:

> *I used to think that saying "good job" was giving feedback to a student. Now I know it is more helpful to give specific feedback about how they can improve.*

And by another teacher who reflected this way:

> *I used to think that giving feedback at the end of a project or test was sufficient. Now I know that it is the feedback I give students during the learning (based on the success criteria) that matters.*

Self- and Peer Assessment

In the US, AfL has routinely been viewed as something that only teachers do: They obtain evidence of learning and adjust their instruction accordingly. More recently, though, as classroom practice has begun to change in response to the introduction of the CCRS and NGSS, with a corresponding focus on learning rather than teaching, student self- and peer assessment are receiving more attention. Indeed, the FAST group revised its definition of *formative assessment* in 2017 and specifically called out self-assessment and peer feedback as essential components of the assessment process (CCSSO, 2018). In addition, an observation protocol to support teacher peer observation and feedback commissioned by the FAST group explicitly includes a rubric for student self-assessment and peer feedback, so teachers can gauge where they are with this practice and decide what they need to do to improve. This protocol is used widely in FAST member states and has been taken up by a number of professional learning providers.

As pointed out in *Inside the Black Box,* self- and peer assessment cannot occur unless students have a clear understanding of the learning targets they are aiming for. While many US teachers still struggle to articulate what is to be learned in a lesson, many others are finding value in being clear with students what they are learning and how they will know if they have learned it. For example, one teacher reported,

> *Now I see assessment for learning as an overarching way of designing lessons so that the goals are very explicit and students are asked to explain where they are with their learning.*

Teachers are also recognizing that self- and peer assessment skills need to be taught and nurtured in their classrooms. Figure 2.1 is an example of a tool from a middle school mathematics lesson that illustrates how the teacher incorporated self-assessment in her classroom. At the end of the lesson, the teacher asked her students to complete an individual assessment of their learning against the success criteria she had established for the lesson (Heritage, 2010, p. 96).

Figure 2.1 Student self-assessment protocol

Think about your learning . . .

Circle the number that you feel best matches your level of success with each item.

I can talk and write about plotting points using correct vocabulary.

Not at all   Absolutely

1   ②   3   4   5

I can plot points in all four quadrants.

Not at all   Absolutely

1   2   3   ④   5

I can create a rule for ordered pairs (x,y) for quadrants I,II,III, and IV.

Not at all   Absolutely

1   ②   3   4   5

After this lesson, I feel like I need more time learning

graphing

_____

_____

_____

_____

She finds that her students are honest about where they think they are in their learning, and she uses their self-assessment along with her own evidence to determine next steps with the students.

Teachers also nurture the development of self-assessment skills by asking students to reflect on their thinking. By making public the value in the ways students are working, teachers enculture students into the practices they want their students to adopt. The excerpt that follows from the end of a middle school mathematics lesson is illustrative of this practice:

> **Teacher:** Pick two or three math practices that you think you engaged in the most today that were the most helpful to you while you did this work, and go ahead and chat with each other about them.
>
> *[Teacher's own reflection: The standards for mathematical practice are tools for the students. These are tools that they need to kind of hone throughout their K–12 experience. If they can do these eight things, they're going to be successful with any kinds of problems. So I want them to really stop and think about their own thinking, what strategies they were using, which math practices were they engaging in that allowed them to be successful with this lesson today.]*
>
> **Teacher:** Michael's group, I heard you guys talking about something good. What was it?
>
> **Student:** Look for and make use of structure.
>
> **Teacher:** So go ahead and find the yellow one, guys—look for and make use of structure. So, Michael, why was structure important in this lesson? What was your group discussing?
>
> **Student:** We were discussing how to find the beginning and um, like, the constant rate of change for each problem.
>
> **Teacher:** So Michael is saying we had to look for important math structures while we were building this function. We had to look for things like rate of change and Y intercept and beginning, and so he said they were examining all those structures to kind of make connections. So, yeah, I think people who make good conjectures use structure really well. (Teaching Channel, n.d.)

With regard to peer assessment, a second-grade teacher describes how she and her partner support the practice in their classrooms:

> Once my students are able to accept the feedback from me, then we move on to peer assessment and feedback, again modeling. We even allow students to come and observe us giving feedback to other students. We allow them to fishbowl in our one-on-one teacher conferences so that they can hear and understand what the process is like. Then we have them practice as peers with one another, giving and receiving feedback and what that is like.

The teacher uses several strategies to help her students understand the nature of giving feedback: She models feedback by providing it to her students, students observe her giving feedback in conferences with individual students, and she provides opportunities for students to practice giving feedback to each other. Peer feedback is not left to chance in her classroom but is carefully nurtured through a variety of strategies.

As educators in the US increasingly recognize the importance of students learning for themselves so that they develop the skills and disposition to learn in school and beyond (e.g., NRC, 2012), we can anticipate that the practice of student self- and peer assessment will become much more prominent in US classrooms.

It is fair to say that AfL has taken hold in the US despite the many obstacles that have been put in its way. It remains to be seen how it will evolve over the next twenty years or so and what the assessment landscape will reveal toward the end of the 2030s.

Two Countries, Two Journeys?

While the impetus and timings of the AfL journeys in the UK and the US may have been different, it is clear that they have many points of similarity. Teachers in both countries have experienced bumps in the road in putting AfL into practice since *Inside the Black Box* first appeared. For example, teachers in the two countries were impacted by policy and legislation in ways that did not always support AfL implementation—for example, high-stakes accountability requirements. Both US and UK teachers had to develop new skills such as providing feedback, and they had to reconsider their role in supporting learning and developing practices that made students more active in their learning and assessment.

Teachers often want to know "what works" in classrooms, but the simple truth is that everything works somewhere, and nothing works everywhere (Wiliam, 2013). Classrooms are far too complex for any recipe to be possible, and the range of contexts across different age groups, backgrounds, and subject disciplines exacerbates this complexity. Nevertheless, AfL provides potential avenues that are worth exploring. Even though AfL requires teachers to reconstruct the way they both think about and enact assessment to boost feedback opportunities within their classroom activities and to take steps to share responsibility for learning with students, many teachers in the UK and the US have been, and continue to be, willing to explore these avenues because they are committed to helping their students be successful learners in school and beyond.

In the next chapter, we focus on how the concept of AfL has expanded since 1998. In particular, we look more closely at the student role in AfL and how student metacognition, self-regulation skills, and growth mindsets are fostered through AfL to support lifelong learning.

REFERENCES

Andrade, H. L., & Heritage, M. (2017). *Using formative assessment to enhance learning, achievement, and academic self-regulation.* New York, NY: Routledge.

Assessment Reform Group. (2002). *Providing constructive responses to learning: Effective feedback—Principles, policy and audit materials.* Cambridge, UK: University of Cambridge.

Black, P., Harrison, C., Lee, C., Marshall, B., & Wiliam, D. (2003). *Assessment for learning: Putting it into practice.* New York, NY: Open University Press.

Black, P., & Wiliam, D. (1998). *Inside the black box: Raising standards through classroom assessment.* London, UK: Department of Education & Professional Studies, King's College London.

Black, P., Wilson, M., & Yao, S. Y. (2011). Road maps for learning: A guide to the navigation of learning progressions. *Measurement: Interdisciplinary Research & Perspective, 9*(2–3), 71–123.

Bloom, B. S. (1956). Taxonomy of educational objectives. *Cognitive Domain*, 120–124.

Blunkett, D. (2000). Raising aspirations for the 21st century. *U.K. Government Blueprint.*

Council of Chief State School Officers. (2018). *Revising the definition of formative assessment.* Washington, DC: Council of Chief State School Officers.

Department for Children, Schools and Families. (2008). *The Assessment for Learning Strategy.* Nottingham, UK: DCSF. Retrieved from www.standards.dfes.gov.uk/secondary/keystage3/all/respub/afl_ws

Department for Education & Science. (2004). *Excellence and enjoyment: Learning and teaching in the primary years—Planning and assessment for learning, assessment for learning, and professional development materials.* London, UK: DfES. Retrieved from https://webarchive.nationalarchives.gov.uk/20040722053413/http://www.dfes.gov.uk/primarydocument/pdfs/DfES-Primary-Ed.pdf

Department for Education. (2015). *Commission on assessment without levels: Final report.* Retrieved from www.gov.uk/government/publications/commission-on- assessment-without-levels-final-report

GovTrack.us. (2019a). H.R.1-107th Congress: No Child Left Behind Act of 2001. Retrieved from https://www.govtrack.us/congress/bills/107/hr1

GovTrack.us. (2019b). S. 1177-114th Congress: Every Student Succeeds Act of 2015. Retrieved from https://www.govtrack.us/congress/bills/114/s1177

Hargreaves, A. (2004). Inclusive and exclusive educational change: Emotional responses of teachers and implications for leadership. *School Leadership and Management, 24*(2), 287–309.

Harrison. C. (2015). Assessment for learning in science classrooms. *Journal of Research in STEM,* 1, 2.

Heritage, M. (2010). *Formative assessment: Making it happen in the classroom.* Thousand Oaks, CA: Corwin.

Heritage, M., & Heritage, J. (2013). Teacher questioning: The epicenter of instruction and assessment. *Applied Measurement in Education, 26*(3), 176–190.

Hodgson, R. (1920). Time, you old gypsy man. In L. Untermeyer (Ed.), *Modern British poetry* (pp. 142–143). New York, NY: Harcourt, Brace and Howe.

Interstate Teacher Assessment and Support Consortium (InTASC). (2011). *InTASC model core teaching standards: A resource for state dialogue.* Washington, DC: Council of Chief State School Officers.

James, M., Black, P., McCormick, R., Pedder, D., & Wiliam, D. (2006). Learning how to learn, in classrooms, schools and networks: Aims, design and analysis. *Research Papers in Education, 21*(2), 101–118.

James, M., McCormick, R., Marshall, B., Pedder, D., & Carmichael, P. (2005, October). *Learning how to learn—In classrooms, schools, and networks* [Research report]. doi:10.13140/2.1.2092.6242

McMillan, J. H. (2013). Why we need research on classroom assessment. In J. McMillan (Ed.), *The SAGE handbook of research on classroom assessment* (pp. 3–16). Thousand Oaks, CA: SAGE.

National Board for Professional Teaching Standards. (2010). *Mathematics standards (3rd edition): For teachers of students ages 11–18+.* Retrieved from http://www.nbpts.org/wp-content/uploads/EAYA-MATH.pdf

National Council of Teachers of Mathematics. (2014). *Principles into actions: Ensuring mathematical success for all.* Reston, VA: Author.

National Governors Association Center for Best Practices, Council of Chief State School Officers. (2010). *Common core state standards.* Washington, DC: Author.

National Research Council. (2000). *How people learn: Brain, mind, experience, and school—Expanded edition.* Washington, DC: The National Academies Press.

National Research Council. (2001). *Knowing what students know: The science and design of educational assessment.* Washington, DC: The National Academies Press.

National Research Council. (2012). *Education for life and work: Developing transferable knowledge and skills in the 21st century*. Washington, DC: The National Academies Press.

Next Generation Science Standards (NGSS) Lead States. (2013). *Next generation science standards: For states, by states*. Washington, DC: The National Academies Press.

Office for Standards in Education. (2008). *Annual report of Her Majesty's Chief Inspector 2006–2007*. London, UK: HMSO.

Office for Standards in Education. (2010). *Annual report of Her Majesty's Chief Inspector 2008–2009*. London, UK: HMSO.

Otero, V. (2006). Moving beyond the "get it or don't" conception of formative assessment. *Journal of Teacher Education, 57*(3), 247–255.

Pellegrino, J. W. (2003). Knowing what students know. *Issues in Science and Technology, 19*(2), 48–52.

Perie, M., Marion, S., & Gong, B. (2009). Moving toward a comprehensive assessment system: A framework for considering interim assessments. *Educational Measurement: Issues and Practice, 28* (3), 5–13.

Perrenoud, P. (1998). From formative evaluation to a controlled regulation of learning: Towards a wider conceptual field. *Assessment in Education: Principles, Policy & Practice, 5*(1), 85–102.

Quality & Curriculum Authority. (2003). *Assessment for Learning: Using assessment to raise achievement in mathematics*. London, UK: Author.

Reay, D., & Wiliam, D. (1999). "I'll be a nothing": Structure, agency and the construction of identity through assessment. *British Educational Research Journal, 25*(3), 343–354.

Rowe, M. B. (1976). Wait time and rewards as instructional variables, their influence on language, logic and fate control. *Journal of Research in Science Teaching, 11*(5), 81–94.

Sadler, D. (1989). Formative assessment and the design of instructional systems. *Instructional Science, 18*, 119–144.

Shepard, L. A. (2000). The role of assessment in a learning culture. *Educational Researcher, 29*(7), 4–14.

Shepard, L. A. (2005). *Formative assessment: Caveat emptor*. Paper presented at the ETS Invitational Conference, The Future of Assessment: Shaping Teaching and Learning, New York, NY.

Shepard, L. A. (2013). Foreword. In J. McMillan (Ed.), *The SAGE handbook of research on classroom assessment* (pp. xix–xxii). Thousand Oaks, CA: SAGE.

Swaffield, S. (2009, September). *The misrepresentation of assessment for learning—and the woeful waste of a wonderful opportunity.* Paper presented at the 20th Annual Conference of the Association for Achievement and Improvement through Assessment (AAIA), Bournemouth, UK.

Teaching Channel. (n.d.). *Transcript for lesson, conjecturing about functions.* Retrieved from https://www.teachingchannel.org/videos/conjecturelessonplan

Wiliam, D. (2013). Assessment: The bridge between teaching and learning. *Voices From the Middle, 21*(2), 15.

Student Role in Assessment for Learning

Black and Wiliam's 1998 review established that assessment for learning (AfL) helps children to learn. So far in this book, we have looked at how AfL provides evidence to help teachers make focused judgments on where children are currently in their learning in order to target next steps and provide the impetus for moving forward. On a daily basis, AfL teachers select and frame activities with a specific purpose in mind and that provide opportunities for their students to learn. Then they monitor what learning is occurring during the lesson by attending to what they see students doing and hear them discussing, as well as from whatever artifact students produce as part of their classroom activities.

All these actions help children learn, but none of them guarantee learning. This is because learning happens inside students' heads and from the sense they make of classroom activities. Learning is individual to students, as they blend and meld new ideas with those that they have already acquired. While AfL tailors teaching to the needs of individual learners and provides opportunities for cognitive growth, moving learning forward requires students to continuously actively engage in the learning process. Simply put, teachers can support learning, but it is the students who actually do the learning—teachers cannot learn for them.

Black and Wiliam's review (1998a, 1998b) acknowledged the role of students in AfL, emphasizing the need to develop students' self- and peer assessment skills; however, their focus was not specifically on the student as learner. This aspect has become much more prominent within our understanding of AfL over the last twenty years, as we have begun to explore how AfL works in a wide variety of classrooms, and has led to an expanded conception of AfL. In this chapter, we focus on the expanded conception of AfL, unpacking how and why AfL supports students in building agency and learning capacity, as well as how underlying theories play a role in creating the classroom climate and teaching approaches that support both learning and agency. Specifically, we will consider how three theoretical perspectives have evolved the thinking about and practice of AfL: (1) sociocultural theory; (2) self-regulated learning; and (3) growth mindset.

Expanding Conceptions of AfL

It may be argued that much of the impetus for expanded conceptions of AfL has been driven by two distinct but related forces. The first is an increased focus on how education needs to respond to the social, economic, and environmental challenges that globalization and technological developments present. As a recent report from the Organization for Economic Cooperation and Development (OECD) about the future of education notes,

> Education has a vital role to play in developing the knowledge, skills, attitudes and values that enable people to contribute to and benefit from an inclusive and sustainable future. Learning to form clear and purposeful goals, work with others with different perspectives, find untapped opportunities and identify multiple solutions to big problems will be essential in the coming years. Education needs to aim to do more than prepare young people for the world of work; it needs to equip students with the skills they need to become active, responsible and engaged citizens. (OECD, 2018, p. 4)

No doubt that the OECD has set a big goal for schools and educators. And commensurate with this big goal is a second force: the increasing recognition that learning opportunities need be broadened so that all students, not just a select few, can achieve high levels of critical, creative, and metacognitive thinking skills, develop the capacity to work with others, and engage in self-reflection about their own learning so that they are prepared both for the world of work and engaged citizenry (National Research Council [NRC], 2012). Consequently, no longer is a narrow, skills-based, didactic approach to learning the order of the day.

In Chapter 2, we noted that a driver in establishing AfL in the US was the report *How People Learn* (HPL, I), published by the National Academies Press (NRC, 2000). Summarizing available findings at the beginning of the 21st century from neuroscience and cognitive science, the report provided insights about learning. A second report that builds on these findings, *How People Learn II*, notes that "what has become far clearer since HPL, I was published is that every individual's learning is profoundly influenced by the particular contexts in which that person is situated (National Academies of Sciences, Engineering & Medicine, 2018, p. 22). This "situative" or sociocultural perspective on learning has gained traction in both the UK and the US, leading to classroom practice in which students learn in collaboration with their teacher and each other to acquire the competencies that the OECD report points to. In turn, sociocultural approaches provide a motivation for AfL to more fully embrace students' participation in their own learning.

Sociocultural Perspective and AfL

Russian psychologist Lev Vygotsky (1962) claimed that the process we call *thinking* develops in children because of their social experiences. His theories stressed that social interaction is fundamental to cognitive development, and he strongly emphasized the context of, and the participants in, the learning process. Ideas about sociocultural approaches to learning stem from Vygotsky's work and have enlarged our view about both the goals of learning and the meaningful participation of students in learning process (Shepard, 2019).

Within a sociocultural perspective, learning takes place through participation in a community of practice (Lave & Wenger, 1991). Learners are apprenticed to the community so that over time they develop expertise through appropriating the community's language, practices, and cultural cues. For instance, students learn how to solve math problems through participating in the discourse and practices of math problem solving, they learn about scientific investigation by participating in the practices and associated science discourse of investigation, and they become a member of a literate community by talking about text with others to access meaning or convey appreciation.

The definition of *AfL* developed at the Third International Conference on Assessment for Learning in 2009 states, "[AfL is] part of everyday practice by students, teachers and peers that seeks, reflects upon and responds to information from dialogue, demonstration and observation in ways that enhance ongoing learning" (cited in Klenowski, 2009, p. 268). Even though Black and Wiliam stressed interaction as the heart of pedagogy, this definition represents a more sociocultural approach to understanding AfL than was apparent in their review for two main reasons: It characterizes both learning and assessment as primarily social activities, which is central to a sociocultural approach, and it includes students as active participants in the learning and assessment process.

In the same vein and subsequent to *Inside the Black Box*, a review of AfL research by Tierney and Charland (2007) concluded that AfL "can be considered a practice that is socially situated as a form of classroom interaction, and historically situated as part of an ongoing theoretical shift in the field of education" (p. 4). When AfL is grounded in sociocultural theory, both teachers and students obtain and use evidence from students' engagement in discourse, active collaboration, and mutually supportive learning opportunities within a community of practice.

The place of feedback in a sociocultural model shifts

> The place of feedback in a sociocultural model shifts learning to a more collaborative view, a dialogue or "loop" where responsibility for learning is shared. This is a significant change to the traditional power and relationship between learner and teacher.

learning to a more collaborative view, a dialogue or "loop" where responsibility for learning is shared. This is a significant change to the traditional power and relationship between learner and teacher. The roles of learner and teacher are shared, and the expertise and experiences of all participants are respected so that "all parties to such a dialogue have an expectation of learning" (Askew & Lodge, 2000, p. 13). For instance, when a teacher provides feedback to a student, the purpose is not to "fix" or "correct" a problem but rather to engage the student's thinking and provide sufficient guidance, without offering a total solution, for the student to take the next steps on his or her own. The teacher can then review how the student has used the feedback and make a determination if more feedback is required or if the student can move on.

Navigating Classroom Complexities

In the reality of the classroom, teachers have to navigate the complexities of their students' learning, continuously adjusting to the "here-and-now circumstances of particular students" (Nuthall, 2007, p. 80). When teachers accept that classrooms are diverse places and that learners are individuals with their own experiences and identities, they can sensitively plan and adapt activities to promote learning. Teachers need to understand that specific topics and activities interest some students and not others, that some students have life experiences that can support particular learning while others do not, and that what one student finds easy may be difficult and confusing for others.

> When teachers accept that classrooms are diverse places and that learners are individuals with their own experiences and identities, they can sensitively plan and adapt activities to promote learning.

How students' own experience and interests shape their learning is illustrated in this excerpt from a lesson on photosynthesis. Monica, who had rarely participated in class discussions in previous lessons, volunteered her emerging ideas about photosynthesis at the start of the class. She raised her hand and explained an event that had occurred over the weekend related to learning about photosynthesis and plant nutrition.

I now know that plants don't suck up food from the soil. I was repotting plants with my gran, and it was really, really difficult getting them out of the pots. They were stuck tight in the soil. The roots are really tight, and there's no gaps. So they can't be getting food from there. It must be from photosynthesis.

Here, Monica is putting together thinking she has done from an experience in her everyday life with the activities and learning that she has been doing in school.

As we see in this example, individuals bring their own personal perspectives and experiences to the interactions within the community, and consequently, there is the possibility of different interpretations of a speaker's statements or of a group's conversations. In using individual interpretations to make sense of a recent conversational history, new or deeper meaning can arise, creating a public resource for any listener in the community to tap into. For example, while other students in the class had not had the same experience as Monica, hearing her explanation of what she thought about photosynthesis and plant nutrition enabled them to consider whether she was providing evidence that fit with their ideas about plant nutrition. In fact, several students nodded as Monica explained her thinking, suggesting they were indeed reconsidering their own thinking. Participation in such interactions is described by Littleton and Mercer (2013) as "interthinking" because it is nested in collaborative learning, which helps students' understanding and so influence achievement. In such a context, AfL pedagogy is crucially concerned with what is salient to students as they engage in discourse and collaboration, as well as with the ways they interpret, make sense, and value the effects of these practices on them as individuals and on others.

Through discussion and sharing ideas, knowledge becomes public in the sociocultural classroom. This means that the teacher not only has the activities that she or he has planned but also the knowledge base of the class to draw on. While diversity might be considered problematic for some in that teachers may be unsure where to pitch the challenges in their lesson, from a sociocultural perspective this situation is not viewed as a deficit model. Instead, the different experiences, knowledge, and values of a diverse class provide a rich mixture of ideas that can be drawn on by students and their teacher, enabling them to consider a greater range of ideas and engage in social relationships to share thinking successfully. In other words, students can become a resource for one another (Heritage, 2007).

Knowing What Is Valued

In a sociocultural perspective, students come to understand what is valued within that subject discipline as they are gradually apprenticed into disciplinary language, skills, and practices. Working out what is valued means that they must pay attention to what expectations and roles are communicated within the classroom through the language of the teacher–student interactions, what learning qualities are privileged, what opportunities are given to participate, and whether the learner judges that she or he has the identity and capacity to participate in a way that will be valued.

An example of how teachers communicate to their students what is valued in the classroom comes from the KMOFAP project described in Chapter 2 (Black et al., 2003). In this project, it was noted by the researchers that teachers' language changed as they adopted AfL pedagogy and that these changes, although small, had a large effect on classroom discussion, allowing and encouraging more student talk and presenting learning as a more negotiated and accumulating event. The illustrative extract that follows is taken from a transcript at the start of a science lesson on photosynthesis with 11-year-old students.

Teacher: *We are going to look at the way plants feed today. I know you've done some work on this in your primary (elementary) school, and I am going to give you time to think that over and to tell your neighbor about what you know—or think you know already.*

[Students start looking at one another and a few whispers are heard.]

Teacher: *Hang on. Not yet. I want to give you something to think about.*

The teacher uses the pronoun *we* in the opening sentence, signaling to students that they have a role to play in taking learning forward and that learning is a negotiated activity involving the teacher and students. They are also acknowledged for bringing experience of this topic from their primary (elementary) school that will be useful in taking ideas forward. While these might seem like small points, they indicate to the students that their teacher values their input and has expectations of their involvement in learning. The teacher then goes on to explain what they are about to engage in and uses the verb *think* three times in this opening sequence. The clear message for students is that thinking is something that the teacher wants them to do, giving value to student ideas and public recognition of these as being important. In fact, the teacher continues using this focus on thinking and student ideas throughout the lesson, sometimes narrating how ideas are being expressed and encouraging learners to contribute their ideas:

| Teacher: | *Richard and Dean think the plant's getting more food. Susan and Stacey as well? Yes. Susan thinks it's because this plant is getting more light. What do others think? Tariq?* |

And sometimes stimulating further thinking:

| Teacher: | *I think I know what Monica and Jamie are getting at, but can anyone put the ideas together? Window? Light? Plants?* |

And also helping students compare and draw ideas together:

| Teacher: | *What do others think about Carolyn's idea?* (Many students nod.) *Yes? It's bigger because it has more light and can photosynthesize more. So, Richard and Dean, how does your idea fit in with this?* |

Working out what is valued can lead to greater participation in learning because students feel they belong within their community of practice and are willing to participate more fully in its activities. In the classroom scenario on photosynthesis, we see how the teacher skillfully encourages and draws learners into the classroom conversation, providing prompts and scaffolding further opportunities for sharing and thinking.

In the next section, we consider self-regulated learning as a more explicit component and outcome of AfL practice.

Self-Regulated Learning

While there are various conceptualizations of self-regulation, most researchers agree that self-regulation enables learners to proactively orient their behaviors to achieving goals (e.g., Boekaerts & Cascallar, 2006; Pintrich, 2004; Zimmerman, 1990). The idea of self-regulation is not a new one. Since the late 1970s and early 1980s, psychologists have been concerned with metacognition—the awareness of and knowledge of one's own thinking and behavior—and how individuals use this knowledge to take action in managing themselves and their learning to achieve goals (Zimmerman, 2002). What is relatively new is the emphasis for students to become lifelong learners through self-regulation so that they can cope and thrive in a rapidly changing world and realize that learning extends long beyond the years of schooling.

Self-regulated learners view learning as an activity they do for themselves in a proactive way rather than as a covert event that happens to them as a reaction to teaching (Zimmerman, 2002). When students are proactive, they are aware of their own thinking, make plans to achieve goals, monitor progress toward those goals, and adjust learning strategies when needed. In short, they develop the skills of learning how to learn.

Teachers can organize their classrooms to provide the structure and learning tools necessary to model and teach self-regulation skills:

- **A positive environment:** The classroom should feel like a safe space where strengths are emphasized and the goals focus on individual improvement. Teachers should model high expectations, make behavioral boundaries clear, and foster positive social relationships within the classroom. This encourages students to pay attention, persevere with tasks, and keep their emotions in check. When a problem behavior occurs, teachers need to figure out why the behavior is occurring and address with the student why it is occurring and what they might do to avoid such behavior in the future.

- **Clear expectations:** Consistency is important. Schedules, procedures, and an established routine help students understand what to expect and create an environment that feels structured and safe.

- **Instruction on study skills:** Students need skills to access and develop disciplinary knowledge; they need to be able to organize their materials, manage their time, stay on task, and retain and practice what is learned in order to be able to engage in later activities. Study skills will help all students to become more independent learners.

AfL and Self-Regulation

Student self-assessment is a necessary practice for self-regulation and was included along with peer assessment in Black and Wiliam's (1998a, 1998b) consideration of AfL. But as self-regulated learning has become more central in education, student autonomy, decision-making, and strategic action have gained in prominence as components of a learning and assessment process. AfL supports students in developing such self-regulatory learning processes through providing opportunities to make decisions about how to use feedback, to set goals from feedback (external feedback from teachers and peers and internal feedback from self-assessment), plan to achieve goals, monitor progress toward those goals, and adjust learning strategies when needed. When students take the initiative and regulate their own learning, they gain deeper insights into how they learn and what works best for them; ultimately, they perform at a higher level (Oettingen, Hönig, & Gollwitzer, 2000; Trentacosta & Izard, 2007).

The social and cultural interactions of the classroom (Cowie, 2005; Elwood, 2008) and teacher and student beliefs about learning and assessment (James & Pedder, 2006) are recognized as having an impact on how learner autonomy, a critical component of self-regulation, is constructed within AfL classroom practices. For instance, Marshall and Drummond (2006) identified that only one fifth of the AfL lessons they observed during the *Learning How to Learn* project promoted learner autonomy, and significantly, they identified that a closed and hierarchical teacher–student relationship constrained autonomy. In classrooms where the authority of the teacher is paramount and where learning is more about acquiring knowledge about what the teacher and others think, rather than learning to think for oneself with teacher guidance and support from peers, then the development of self-regulatory processes is inevitably limited or even nonexistent. It's hardly surprising that the importance of working within a sociocultural context emerged as an important theme from their research.

Changes in Classroom Relationships

In a sociocultural context, instead of the vertical relationships being prevalent, as for example, when teachers do all the talking (i.e., transmit information) and students take a test at the end of a period of instruction and are only informed of their results, horizontal relationships in which students collaborate with teachers and their peers to make decisions about their own learning predominate (Heritage, 2017). In the following example, we can see how one teacher advanced self-regulatory skills within a sociocultural context, characterized by horizontal relationships.

Maria was planning a unit on design and technology for her class of 9-year-old students in which their aim was to design, produce, and decorate a jewelry box. Maria suspected that many of her class would focus more on the decoration than the construction of the box, so she wanted to convey to her students the high value she was putting on the construction aspect of the task. Maria's concern was how to model this value, so she considered opportunities of how to achieve this goal.

She began by discussing her planning with a colleague, Aisha, who had taught the same unit to her class earlier in the year. Aisha confirmed Maria's concern that decoration of the box had taken priority over construction in her class, and the two teachers hit on an idea to hopefully change the thinking of the children in Maria's class. Aisha asked her class to bring in the jewelry boxes they had made earlier in the year so that Maria's students could see what they looked like and the condition the boxes were now in after some four months of use. Twelve students in Aisha's class brought their jewelry boxes; the other children either forgot or had given the boxes as presents or their boxes had, sadly, been thrown away.

The following day, Maria set up a display of the twelve boxes in the middle of the room and asked her class to walk around and take a good look at the boxes. They were able to pick them up carefully and look inside and were encouraged to discuss freely with others what they thought of each box. After five minutes, Maria grouped the children into threes and asked them to discuss and select the best three boxes, giving reasons for their selection. Following this, Maria conducted a whole-class discussion in which she collected the reasons for each group's choice. In all, five boxes were selected, two of them appearing in everyone's top three and three others fitting in several groups' top three.

The criteria that the groups came up with for deciding on the quality of the box were as follows:

1. Whether the lid fit the box evenly

2. Whether the hinges worked to open and close the lid

3. How sturdy and secure the joints were on the five pieces of the box

4. Whether the depth of the box was sufficient to fit jewelry in

5. How colorful and creative the box covering was

While the decoration of the box was seen as important to the students, as it turned out it was only one of five criteria for quality. Viewing the finished products, borrowed from Aisha's class, enabled Maria's students to understand more clearly what they needed to do to produce their own box.

The approach that Maria took was a sociocultural one in that she created the opportunity for the children to discuss their ideas about the completed boxes and then to plan how they might achieve the construction of their own jewelry box. The criteria generated through class discussion were then used by the students to monitor their own progress as they began construction. At times when Maria was demonstrating how to secure the pieces of the box together or how to fit the lid, most of the students focused carefully on what she was showing them and, later in the activity, independently came up to her and checked on particular aspects before making their own attempts at construction. In this way, children were targeting what they needed to do to achieve quality in their work.

When the boxes were complete, Maria asked children to self-assess their own boxes against the five criteria and then to seek validation of what they had done well and where there were areas for improvement from their peers. Overall, the quality of the boxes that Maria's class produced were of a higher quality than Aisha's class, but more important, all children completed the task, whereas three in Aisha's class had given up and had boxes without lids or decoration. The children were motivated and persevered, even when they sometimes made mistakes and had to redo parts of the construction. The other difference between the two classes was that Maria's students had language to evaluate their final product and justify to others their achievement while still recognizing they had future targets.

A nonsociocultural approach to this unit, characterized by a hierarchical vertical relationship between teacher and the students, would likely have gone something like this: The teacher tells the students what the criteria are, the students construct the boxes according to the criteria, the teacher makes a judgment about the quality of the products, and then the teacher awards marks, a grade, or a score. Maria's classroom operates much more on the basis of horizontal relationships in which students are supported to develop self-regulatory skills. As we saw in Maria's classroom example, AfL practices foster self-regulation to the extent that they encourage students to focus on their actions throughout the learning process, including

- before the learning task has begun, when the student can consider the task, set goals, and develop a plan to accomplish the task;

- during the task, when the student must monitor his or her own performance and see how well various strategies work;

- after the task, when the students can reflect on their performance and determine what worked well, what didn't, and what needs to change.

Learner Agency

In an AfL classroom, all students need to be active in their learning—willing to share and listen to ideas, as well as be responsive to feedback and determined to learn. Understanding how to "play the game" (Gee, 2004) and when to enact permission is also known in the literature as "learner agency." Individuals with high levels of agency have the capacity to take purposeful initiative, do not respond passively to their circumstances, and seek to achieve the conditions they desire in their own and others' lives (Vander Ark, 2015). The qualities of agency do not represent a fixed state, but rather a potential state, and the role of an autonomous learner can only be fulfilled within social relationships (Ratner, 2000). The skills, language, and behavior associated with the role of an autonomous learner are given legitimacy within a community of practice in overt as well as oblique ways (Van Leeuwen, 2007). Key aspects of the classroom cultures where autonomy develops include encouragement of high self-responsibility in learning, distributed expertise, socially constructed knowledge, learning proceeding from action, and trust among group members, such that the cost of errors is small (Perry, VandeKamp, Mercer, &

> In an AfL classroom, all students need to be active in their learning—willing to share and listen to ideas, as well as be responsive to feedback and determined to learn.

Nordby, 2002). These practices seem to position students as active, responsible, autonomous learners.

To illustrate how these practices look in action, we turn to an example of a fourth-grade history class. The students in this class are apprenticed to the discipline of history. They work from primary source (firsthand) materials to analyze and draw inferences about particular time periods in the past. The students are encouraged to think like historians and detectives, to look for clues, read closely, use background knowledge, contextualize source information, corroborate, read the silences, and notice and document the stories the primary sources are telling (Wineburg, 2010). In this particular lesson, students were focusing on primary source documents that represented different people living or moving to California over different periods of California history. Working in groups, each student was asked to take one of the sources, describe the perspectives of the people, and infer what the sources represent or communicate. Then they were to share their observations with their group peers and discuss how the various sources connect and, together, what story they tell. Finally, the group had to come up with three questions that they would want to ask the people in their sources and why, which each group then shared with the entire class in turn. As the students were discussing their ideas, the teacher was conferring with individuals and groups, recording the students' observations and inferences, which were used in the final whole-class discussion to focus the students' thinking more deeply around the ideas of movement, patterns, perspectives, and connections.

In this example, the students were given legitimacy in their community of practice as historians; they were given responsibility in learning, not just for themselves but for others, too. Their expertise was distributed because each student had to contribute his or her analysis and inferences to the group, and they constructed knowledge collectively from these individual contributions. Learning proceeded from joint action and trust—each student trusted other group members to provide their perspective on the source document, and the teacher trusted the students to use these individual perspectives to come to a collective view about the story that was being told.

Self-regulatory practices can go a long way to helping students take action and believe in their own capabilities, but there are still times when some students are devastated by setbacks in their learning, while other students take setbacks in their stride. This differing response among students was studied by Carol Dweck, who coined the terms *fixed* and *growth mindsets* to describe the different underlying beliefs students have about learning and intelligence, which are closely related to students' sense of autonomy. This aspect is considered in more detail in the next section.

Growth Mindsets

The motivations and self-perceptions of students and their assessment histories are important influences on how they receive feedback (Deci & Ryan, 1994). Carol Dweck (2000) brings this to the fore in her conception of "mindsets." In her research, Dweck (2000) identified two sets of beliefs that individuals can have about their own intelligence. They may have a "fixed mindset" in which they believe that intelligence is a fixed trait—some people are smart, some are not, and that's just the way it is. Or they may have a "growth mindset" in which they believe that their intellectual ability can develop. All students are on a continuum between these two states depending on the task, context, and their educational histories. For instance, girls may be led to believe that they are no good at science or mathematics, which in turn affects how they see themselves as capable learners who can develop their abilities in these areas. Similarly, they may believe that girls are good at reading and writing, priming them to be more inclined to these subjects. Students who believe that intelligence can be developed are more willing to invest effort in learning, are more self-confident, and are better able to deal effectively with setbacks.

The feedback teachers give students can influence their mindsets in surprising ways. For example, while praise for "smartness" is considered by some teachers to be motivating, research demonstrates that it can actually have a negative impact on student motivation and achievement. For example,

> Students who believe that intelligence can be developed are more willing to invest effort in learning, are more self-confident, and are better able to deal effectively with setbacks.

in a study with fifth graders, Mueller and Dweck (1998) put students into two groups to work on a puzzle task. One group, after succeeding initially, was praised for its intelligence and ability. The other group, also after succeeding, was praised for its effort. As the tasks became more challenging, the groups reacted in very different ways.

Students praised for smartness elected to continue working on the easier tasks, while students praised for effort chose to progress to more challenging tasks. Smart students were averse to failure, whereas those students praised for effort realized they could learn from their mistakes and make progress. When students were praised for intelligence, they came to attribute their success to a fixed quality of themselves, while students praised for effort believed that their performance could be improved if they continued to work on the task.

A growth mindset is linked with resilience, confidence, and task completion. In a growth mindset, students believe that their most basic capabilities can be developed through dedication and hard work rather than relying on natural talent. They respond well to feedback and are generally keen to take on and apply new strategies, building a repertoire of ways to support their own learning.

A fixed mindset usually results from a continual focus on performance and ability rather than on effort and achievement. It encourages students to compare themselves with others, so they come to see themselves as successful or failures with particular disciplines or skills. In severe cases, this results in what Dweck terms *self-helplessness*, where students see their failures as an inevitable trait and they tell others that they cannot write creatively or do math or play a sport. In reality, they are in protection mode, avoiding challenge, hiding away from mistakes, and judging constructive criticism as a reason to opt out and quit.

Encouraging Growth Mindsets

The difficulty for teachers is that much of the feedback happens in the public arena of the classroom, and one learner's success may signal to others that they are unsuccessful. Teachers therefore need to think about the values they encourage and the language they use to embed classroom behaviors that are conducive to all students developing growth mindsets. In a growth mindset culture, a learner's progress, rather than a high performance, should be celebrated verbally and personally, with the focus on the steps that got the student to that point. Perhaps the most significant aspect here is how praise is used. Dweck's ideas suggest that teachers use praise such as "Everyone is smart!" or in the face of failure, "Great effort! You tried your best" (Dweck, 2015, p. 2). Instead of a focus on the individual, it should be focused on the process as part of classroom routines to do the metacognitive work of asking what strategies have been tried and what might be helpful to try next (Shepard, 2019).

> In a growth mindset culture, a learner's progress, rather than a high performance, should be celebrated verbally and personally, with the focus on the steps that got the student to that point.

Focusing on development is also useful, so adding the word *yet* to the end of the sentence, when children claim they cannot manage the perfect tense in Spanish or solve simultaneous equations, indicates to learners that they need to persevere, practice, and find new strategies to continue learning. Alternatively, providing reasons for encouraging another attempt can help—for example, suggesting that every time they practice, they are making the connections in their brain stronger or having analogies such as "the brain is sometimes like a muscle that you need to regularly exercise and challenge it to keep it functioning."

AfL and a growth mindset go hand-in-hand. They both focus on improvement, making efforts to improve, and active participation in learning. Unless teachers believe that all students can improve on their current achievement, they will not be able to target appropriate challenges and opportunities for all students to improve. And unless students are encouraged to believe that they can become smarter with guidance, support, and effort, they will likely not achieve levels of success that are potentially within their grasp.

> *AfL and a growth mindset go hand-in-hand. They both focus on improvement, making efforts to improve, and active participation in learning.*

Since the 1998 publication of *Inside the Black Box*, the conception of AfL has broadened. In this chapter, we have examined how three theoretical perspectives have contributed to the expanded conceptions of AfL. These theoretical perspectives are not new. Vygotsky's theories were first published in Russian in the 1920s, introduced to the English-speaking world in translation in 1962, and subsequently stimulated other leading theoretical perspectives that we have highlighted in this chapter (e.g., situative/sociocultural, apprenticeship, community of practice), as well as increased emphasis on interaction as a means to learn. We noted earlier that ideas of self-regulation have been present in the psychological literature since the 1970s and 1980s, and Carol Dweck developed her theories and tested them empirically in the 1980s (e.g., Dweck, 1986; Dweck & Leggett, 1988).

As teachers across the world have implemented AfL, the affordances of these theoretical perspectives for both improved learning and assessment have become increasingly salient, amplified by societal demands for students to develop the competencies for lifelong learning and engaged citizenry. The inclusion of these theoretical perspectives within the conceptualization of practice of AfL has significantly impacted how teachers teach and how students learn. Students are actively involved in their own learning and assessment, they are apprenticed into disciplinary learning within a community of practice in collaboration with their teacher and peers, they engage in discourse with each other and their teacher, they have much greater agency in learning, and they are encouraged to believe that with effort and perseverance they can accomplish challenging learning goals.

In the next chapter, we will go into detail about how teachers can plan for learning and assessment within this broader conceptualization of AfL.

REFERENCES

Askew, S., & Lodge, C. (2000). Gifts, ping-pong and loops-linking feedback and learning. In S. Askew (Ed.), *Feedback for learning* (pp. 1–17). London, UK: RoutledgeFalmer.

Black, P., Harrison, C., Lee, C., Marshall, B., & William, D. (2003). *Assessment for learning: Putting it into practice*. Maidenhead, UK: Open University Press.

Black, P., & Wiliam, D. (1998a). Assessment and classroom learning. *Assessment in Education: Principles, Policy & Practice, 5*(1), 7–74.

Black, P., & Wiliam, D. (1998b). *Inside the black box: Raising standards through classroom assessment*. London, UK: Department of Education & Professional Studies, King's College London.

Boekaerts, M., & Cascallar, E. (2006). How far have we moved toward the integration of theory and practice in self-regulation? *Educational Psychology Review, 18*(3), 199–210.

Cowie, B. (2005). Pupil commentary on assessment for learning. *The Curriculum Journal, 16*(2), 137–151.

Deci, E. L., & Ryan, R. M. (1994). Promoting self determined education. *Scandinavian Journal of Educational Research, 38*(1), 3–14.

Dweck, C. S. (1986). Motivational processes affecting learning. *American Psychologist, 41*(10), 1040–1048.

Dweck, C. S. (2000). *Self-theories: Their role in motivation, personality, and development*. Philadelphia, PA: Psychology Press.

Dweck, C. S. (2015, September 23). Carol Dweck revisits the "growth mindset." *Education Week*. Retrieved from http://edweek.org/ew/articles/2015/09/23/carol-dweck-revisits-the-growth-mindset.html

Dweck, C. S., & Leggett, E. L. (1988). A social–cognitive approach to motivation and personality. *Psychological Review, 95*(2), 256–273.

Ellwood, C. (2008). Questions of classroom identity: What can be learned from codeswitching in classroom peer group talk? *The Modern Language Journal, 92*(4), 538–557.

Gee, J. P. (2004). *An introduction to discourse analysis: Theory and method*. New York, NY: Routledge.

Heritage, M. (2007). Formative assessment: What do teachers need to know and do? *Phi Delta Kappan, 89*(2), 140–145.

Heritage, M. (2017). Changing the assessment relationship to empower teachers and students. In K. L. McClarty, K. D. Mattern, & M. N. Gaertner (Eds.), *Preparing students for college and careers: Theory, measurement, and educational practice*. New York, NY: Routledge.

James, M., & Pedder, D. (2006). Beyond method: Assessment and learning practices and values. *The Curriculum Journal*, *17*(2), 109–138.

Klenowski, V. (2009). Assessment for learning revisited: An Asia-Pacific perspective. *Assessment in Education: Principles, Policy & Practice*, *16*(3), 263–268.

Lave, J., & Wenger, E. (1991). *Situated learning: Legitimate peripheral participation*. Cambridge, UK: Cambridge University Press.

Littleton, K., & Mercer, N. (2013). *Interthinking: Putting talk to work*. Abingdon-on-Thames, UK: Routledge.

Marshall, B., & Drummond, M. J. (2006). How teachers engage with assessment for learning: Lessons from the classroom. *Research Papers in Education*, *21*(2), 133–149.

Mueller, C. M., & Dweck, C. S. (1998). Praise for intelligence can undermine children's motivation and performance. *Journal of Personality and Social Psychology*, *75*(1), 33.

National Academies of Sciences, Engineering & Medicine. (2018). *How people learn II: Learners, contexts and cultures*. Washington, DC: The National Academies Press.

National Research Council. (2000). How people learn: Brain, mind, experience, and school. J. D. Bransford, A. L. Brown, & R. R. Cocking (Eds.), *Committee on Developments in the Science of Learning, Commission on Behavioral and Social Sciences and Education, National Research Council*. Washington, DC: National Academy Press.

National Research Council. (2012). *Education for life and work: Developing transferable knowledge and skills in the 21st century*. Washington, DC: The National Academies Press.

Nuthall, G. (2007). *The hidden lives of learners*. Wellington, New Zealand: NZCER Press.

Oettingen, G., Hönig, G., & Gollwitzer, P. M. (2000). Effective self-regulation of goal attainment. *International Journal of Educational Research*, *33*(7–8), 705–732.

Organization for Economic Cooperation and Development. (2018). *The future of education and skills: Education 2030*. Paris, France: Author.

Perry, N. E., VandeKamp, K. O., Mercer, L. K., & Nordby, C. J. (2002). Investigating teacher–student interactions that foster self-regulated learning. *Educational Psychologist*, *37*(1), 5–15.

Pintrich, P. R. (2004). A conceptual framework for assessing motivation and self-regulated learning in college students. *Educational Psychology Review*, *16*(4), 385–407.

Ratner, C. (2000). Agency and culture. *Journal for the Theory of Social Behaviour*, *30*(4), 413–434.

Shepard, L. A. (2019). Classroom assessment to support teaching and learning. In A. Berman, M. J. Feuer, & J. W. Pellegrino (Eds.), *The Annals of the American Academy of Political and Social Science* (pp. 183–200). Thousand Oaks, CA: SAGE.

Tierney, R. D., & Charland, J. (2007, April). *Stocks and prospects: Research on formative assessment in secondary classrooms.* Paper presented at the annual meeting of the American Educational Research Association, Chicago, IL.

Trentacosta, C. J., & Izard, C. E. (2007). Kindergarten children's emotion competence as a predictor of their academic competence in first grade. *Emotion, 7*(1), 77.

Van Leeuwen, T. (2007). Legitimation in discourse and communication. *Discourse & Communication, 1*(1), 91–112.

Vander Ark, T. (2015). Ten tips for developing student agency. Retrieved from https://www.gettingsmart.com/2015/12/201512tips-for-developing-student-agency/

Vygotsky, L. S. (1962). *Thought and language* (E. Hanfmann & G. Vakar, Trans.). Cambridge, MA: MIT Press.

Wineburg, S. (2010). Thinking like a historian. *Library of Congress TPS Quarterly*. Retrieved from http://www.loc.gov/teachers/tps/quarterly/historical_thinking/article.html

Zimmerman, B. J. (1990). Self-regulated learning and academic achievement: An overview. *Educational psychologist, 25*(1), 3–17.

Zimmerman, B. J. (2002). Becoming a self-regulated learner: An overview. *Theory Into Practice, 41*(2), 64–70.

Planning for Learning

> *My planning has changed a lot. Instead of being focused on the activity and what I am going to say, I'm focusing on what the students are learning and what they are doing with the learning. I also think through what they might not understand and how I could question in a way to help push them toward understanding as opposed to me presenting information and students passively consuming it.*
>
> Fourth-grade US teacher

The quote that begins this chapter is a reflection by a fourth-grade teacher after a period of focusing on AfL in her classroom. What we learn is how her practice has changed to center on learning rather than teaching and the effect of this change on her planning. Her quote echoes Black and Wiliam's view from *Inside the Black Box* that when teachers accept the evidence that a transmission model of learning does not work, they are willing to commit to teaching through interaction, building a classroom culture of questioning and deep thinking in which students learn from shared discussions with teachers and peers. In such a classroom, AfL can thrive.

In *Inside the Black Box,* Black and Wiliam (1998b) stressed the importance of classroom tasks in teacher planning, both in terms of the learning aims that they serve and the opportunities for students to communicate their evolving understanding—for example, through discussion, teacher observation, and careful listening to student talk. Such opportunities for students to express their understanding "should be designed into any piece of teaching" (Black & Wiliam, 1998b, p. 11). As Black and Wiliam make clear, planning for learning and AfL together are indivisible, a recognition expressed by the fourth-grade teacher in her quote. In this chapter, we explore planning for learning and AfL, along with how teachers in the UK and the US have developed their practice in this regard since *Inside the Black Box* pointed the way, and discuss the influences that have shaped their development. We begin by considering two distinct approaches to teaching and learning.

Distinct Teaching Approaches

It is likely that we have all seen, or even been recipients of, a teaching approach characterized by teacher talk, student listening (hopefully), and tests aimed at checking that students have learned what they were supposed to. This approach can be considered a "transmission model," referenced in *Inside the Black Box*, through which teachers transmit learning to the students, disseminating information, rather than assisting students to construct ideas and develop their own thinking. In "transmission" teaching, lesson planning takes the form of prescribing a fixed sequence of tasks, and assessment is focused on correctness and accuracy. This approach to teaching and learning ignores much well-established cognitive theory and research—for example, the active involvement of the student in the learning process, the social aspects of learning, and metacognitive thinking (Black, Wilson, & Yao, 2011).

AfL represents a different approach because it requires the teacher to focus on the students' learning rather than on the curriculum demands. Common to all AfL practice is the active involvement of students, whose role changes from passive recipients of knowledge to active partners in the learning process (Swaffield, 2011). Students find out what makes sense and develop ideas through self- and peer critique that also encourage next steps in learning. In this context, teachers have to decide which of the many diverse student ideas and experiences are productive starting points for developing learning. Given the dynamic assessment information that accrues in AfL, the teacher can decide how to respond to their students' current conceptual understanding of a particular topic. Students can use feedback from their teacher to evaluate their own and others' work, learn from their mistakes, and learn to reflect on their own learning. The goal of AfL is not, however, to eliminate mistakes but rather to keep them from becoming chronic (Stiggins, 2007) so that they do not interfere with the development and progression of ideas.

In their extended review of studies of formative assessment practice, from which *Inside the Black Box* is derived, Black and Wiliam concluded that implementing AfL cannot be accomplished by teachers making marginal changes in classroom work. Instead, it involves deep changes in teachers' classroom practice and their role in relation to their students. Implementing AfL would require teachers to make more than marginal changes in their classroom practice (Black & Wiliam, 1998a). One of the deep changes for many teachers is their lesson planning and preparation. AfL has more chance of prospering when teachers move to an approach in which the social aspects of learning are promoted and students are actively involved in constructing their

> *Implementing AfL cannot be accomplished by teachers making marginal changes in classroom work. Instead, it involves deep changes in teachers' classroom practice and their role in relation to their students.*

own understanding with teacher support. This necessary change is well summed up by a sixth-grade mathematics teacher when she observed that *"formative assessment has changed me as a teacher and has changed my students as learners"* (Heritage, 2010, p. 2). Her comment arises from the fundamental changes she made in her teaching and her invitations to students to be actively involved in their own learning.

With respect to changes in planning for teaching and learning, let us elaborate further by reference to a publication from the National Council of Teachers of Mathematics (NCTM, 2014). This publication describes the changes in teaching and learning, specifically in mathematics, needed to achieve college and career readiness standards (CCRS), introduced in every state in the US over the last several years. NCTM advocates for changes from the traditional lesson paradigm, which features "review, demonstration and practice" (NCTM, 2014, p. 9), to lessons that promote deeper thinking and reasoning about mathematics and discussion with others, which in the process, "design" AfL opportunities into the lesson. For example, students engage in "using and connecting mathematical representations," which for planning purposes involves teachers in "selecting tasks that allow students to decide which representations to use in making sense of the problem; and allocating substantial instructional time for students to use, discuss, and make connections among representations" (NCTM, 2014, p. 9). During the lesson, students are engaged in "using multiple forms of representations to make sense of and understand mathematics; and describing and justifying their mathematical understanding and reasoning with drawings, diagrams, and other representations" (NCTM, 2014, p. 29). As Black and Wiliam suggested, the AfL opportunities of observation and listening to students express their thinking are built in to the learning tasks as they use representations to understand mathematics and describe and justify their understanding and reasoning. Teachers are able to respond to student thinking while it unfolds so as to continuously progress learning, a practice characterized by the fourth-grade teacher as helping *"to push them [the students] toward understanding."*

The changes advocated by NCTM to reach CCRS goals are salient to other disciplines as well; teachers are required to create rich learning tasks and activities that are interactive, enable learners to engage in their own sensemaking, and provide opportunities to explain their thinking. When lesson planning reflects these features, opportunities for AfL are integrated into the learning tasks and activities.

One secondary history teacher explained his approach to planning for learning in this way:

> *I think through first which sort of activities fit with current learning aims in the topic, and I adapt these (activities) with a range of students in mind. How might those who were struggling with these ideas last time be helped? How might those who easily picked up ideas be stretched? Are*

there particular issues or opportunities I need to be aware of? You can't plan for all eventualities, but framing the lesson with your learners in mind gives you enough shape and scope to make it a likely success in terms of learning.

These changes in planning are echoed by teachers in both the US and the UK:

I used to think that formative assessment was something extra that had to be added to a lesson or another quiz to give to determine how well students were learning. But now I know that formative assessment is an underlying part of the lesson, strategically and purposefully related to how I interact with my students and how my students interact with their learning. (US teacher)

I used to think that formative assessment was just checking for understanding, but now I think it is an integral part of a lesson plan and essential to reaching learning goals. (US teacher)

AfL is central to what I do. It's what I pin my lesson activities onto and what my students look for in terms of supporting their own learning. (UK teacher)

Much of our own work with teachers has focused on lesson planning for AfL. In the following section, we describe some of the tools we have found useful in supporting teachers' thinking and planning processes.

Lesson Planning Tools

Figure 4.1 shows a template that Margaret has used extensively with US teachers to assist their planning for learning and AfL. As already noted, students in the US are required to meet CCRS, so the focus of any lesson is a chunk of learning positioned in a longer trajectory of learning toward the standards. This chunk forms a learning goal for the lesson, and teachers either describe or co-construct success criteria with students—indicators of what meeting the goal entails. The opportunities for learning are designed to embody the learning goal and the success criteria, and teachers are asked to think about the formative assessment opportunities embedded in the learning experiences. They are also aware that if they cannot identify ways to obtain evidence during the learning, they need to go back to the drawing board and start over! The final step in the planning is to think in advance about the kinds of questions they might ask—for example, to either promote discussion or to probe student thinking in one-on-one or small group interactions. Teachers are also encouraged to anticipate student responses so that they can be prepared with appropriate actions to support their learning

Figure 4.1 Lesson Planning Template

Standard(s)

Learning Goal(s)	**Success Criteria**

Tasks/activities/strategies to help students meet the learning goal

Formative opportunities in tasks/activities/strategies to gather evidence of student learning

Questions to gather evidence of student learning

Anticipated responses

Figure 4.2 Completed Lesson Planning Template

Standard(s)
Describe how words and phrases (e.g., regular beats, alliteration, rhymes, lines) supply rhythm and meaning in a story, poem, or song.

Learning Goal	**Success Criteria**
Understand how poetic devices supply rhythm and meaning in a poem	*Identify the poetic device used in the poem. Explain how the device supplies rhythm and meaning*

Tasks/activities/strategies to help students meet the learning goal
Mini lesson on alliteration—class read and pairs discussion on the purpose and effect of alliteration in the poem.
Individual reading of poems; complete response Post-it _____
I noticed the poet used _____. The poet used _____ because _____.

Formative opportunities in tasks/activities/strategies to gather evidence of student learning
Whole class discussion of alliteration
Listening in to pairs discussion
Review of Post-it responses on the response board
Individual reading conferences with students (Jules, Jaime, Alexandra, Miguel, Julia)

Questions to gather evidence of student learning
What is the purpose of alliteration in this poem? What is the effect the poet creates? How is this device similar to or different from others we have learned about? What poetic device is the poet using in the poem you are reading? Why do you think the poet chose this device? What effect do you think it has on the poem? (Look out for confusions among devices, as well as confusions between rhythm and meaning.)

Figure 4.2 shows a completed planning template for a second-grade English language arts lesson. As you can see, the teacher has designed learning tasks in which AfL opportunities are available.

Figures 4.3 and 4.4 show the style of the AfL Lesson Planning Sheet that Chris has used to help teachers shape and scope their lesson. While teachers may then use the planning sheet to complete lesson planning protocols specific for their school, the AfL Lesson Planning Sheet helps the teachers focus on and generate the purpose and drive of the lesson through the professional thinking that occurs to construct and refine the lesson's objectives, organization, and questions. By ensuring these three aspects are clear, teachers can then be aware of where the formative opportunities lie in their lesson and be able to make good use of these through the questions and prompts they have planned.

While changing teacher practice is challenging (e.g., Windschitl, 2002), many teachers in both the UK and the US have made significant shifts in the ways they think about planning for learning and for AfL. Since the publication of *Inside the Black Box,* various developments in the education landscape of both countries have influenced teacher practice in positive directions. Next, we describe some of those developments and how they have shaped teacher practice to be more amenable to AfL implementation.

Figure 4.3   AfL Lesson Planning Template

Lesson Topic

Setting the Scene for Learning
How will you introduce the thinking and approach needed in this lesson?

Lesson Objectives
How do you communicate your objectives and expectations to the students? Success criteria?

Stimulus Material
How will you focus and prompt thinking and ideas? What resources will you need? What questions will you need?

Instruction and Formative Opportunities
How will you organize and manage activities and links? What resources will you need? What questions will you need?

Reflection
How will you help students realize what they have achieved, what progress they have made, and where they need to focus next?

Figure 4.4 Completed Lesson Planning Template.

Lesson Topic
Using musical features to demonstrate emotion

Setting the Scene for Learning
Today, we are looking at different musical styles. The reason for this is that later you will use one style in your own composition to display or reflect a particular emotion. What we are looking for in your piece is a clear style being used to reflect melancholy and a clear explanation of why you have chosen that style.

Lesson Objectives
To develop a two-minute composition to reflect an emotion.
To explain how and why the composition style conveys a specific emotion.

Stimulus Material
Matching music clips with art images:
Which emotions are conveyed by each of the art images?
Which music clip fits each art image best? Discuss why you feel this.
Dictionary definitions of melancholy.
Imagine a film scene that displays a melancholy event and think about the music background.

Instruction and Formative Opportunities
In explaining an emotion, attitude, or value, the issue of judgment is important. This is often about opinion and is different from fact. These types of explanation about your emotions, values, or attitudes should feature the notion of opinion with justification that is relating to some form of evidence.

- *Model the process of planning an explanation for joy (Picture A and Music Clip 2)*
- *Composition time*
- *Sharing and explaining composition in pairs*
- *Critiquing compositions in pairs—which parts work well?*
- *What are the musical features that make it work well for this emotion?*
- *Where might improvements or alternatives be tried?*

Reflection
What did we learn today about creating and explaining emotion in composition? How would you plan to produce a composition on anger?

Influences on Changing Practice

This section focuses on three main influences: (1) the effects of policy decisions; (2) a renewed focus on AfL in the disciplines; and (3) the increased use of professional learning communities for teacher development.

The Effects of Policy Decisions

As we have noted, most jurisdictions in the US have adopted CCRS and Next Generation Science Standards (NGSS), which lay out grade-level achievement expectations for students and represent more demanding goals than many previous state standards. The mathematics CCRS require a balance between conceptual understanding and procedural fluency and the ability to connect these two types of knowledge. Mathematic practices require students to reason abstractly and quantitatively, construct viable arguments and critique the reasoning of others, and communicate their reasoning about concepts (Moschkovich, 2012). In English language arts (English), CCRS call for students to engage with complex texts to build knowledge across the curriculum; use evidence to inform, argue, and analyze; work collaboratively to understand multiple perspectives and present ideas; and develop and use the linguistic resources to do all of these (Bunch, Kibler, & Pimental, 2012). The NGSS require students to ask questions, plan and carry out investigations, analyze and interpret data, construct explanations, engage in argument from evidence, and obtain, evaluate, and communicate information (Lee, Quinn, & Valdés, 2013).

The introduction of CCRS and NGSS has necessitated many teachers making considerable changes in their teaching approach, specifically adopting "ambitious teaching practices" (Lampert et al., 2013; Windschitl, Thompson, & Braaten, 2011) that are discourse-based, permit students to think deeply and to respond to each other's thinking, allow students extensive opportunities to explain their reasoning, and gain experience with specific aspects of disciplinary practices. Such teaching practices are entirely consistent with those envisaged in *Inside the Black Box* that afford opportunities for AfL: an interactive model of learning that allows students to express their reasoning and understanding, as well as engage with teachers and each other in thoughtful, reflective dialogue focused on evoking and exploring understanding so that all students have an opportunity to think. Alas, pedagogy in the US twenty years ago when *Inside the Black Box* was first published did not generally reflect ambitious teaching in ways that assisted AfL. But fortunately, times do change.

The research literature on ambitious teaching practices arose more than a decade ago, primarily in the area of teacher preparation, so that beginning teachers would have the skills needed to support all students in reaching the demanding learning goals laid out by CCRS and NGSS (Shepard, 2019). It is not difficult to imagine the challenge for teachers who practice a primarily "transmission" model approach to incorporate collaborative and investigative opportunities for their students that permit them to do what CCRS and NGSS require. Without adopting ambitious teaching practices, even veteran teachers will likely find it a challenge to meet the standards. Therefore, ambitious teaching has become increasingly salient for all classroom teachers, and the benefits accruing to AfL are significant.

When teachers plan lessons with learning opportunities concomitant with the requirements of the standards and ambitious teaching, the potential to make students' thinking visible—for example, through their explanations and justifications about their reasoning, their representations of ideas in models and writing—is enhanced.

The following veteran eighth-grade mathematics teacher's observation on her approach to teaching conjecturing about functions required by the CCRS is illustrative of her move to more ambitious teaching:

> *Like generalizing, conjecturing relies on the ability to extend the reasoning beyond the domain that started the conversation to begin with. This represents a tremendous shift in my teaching. We used to just represent functions in four ways and solve problems. And while we still do this, we do it for a reason—we are constantly looking to conjecture and generalize. This leads naturally to investigating why and will end with either justification or something that has been refuted . . . and we start again.* (Teaching Channel, n.d.)

The "shift" she describes in her teaching provides many opportunities for AfL during her lesson through the students' representations, justifications, and refutations. It is fair to say that the introduction of CCRS and NGSS prepared a fertile ground for AfL, which many US teachers and those who support them have subsequently capitalized on.

In the UK, the influence of the introduction of a new National Curriculum in 2015 created fresh challenges as teachers were told that they needed to

> set high expectations for every pupil. They should plan stretching work for pupils whose attainment is significantly above the expected standard. They have an even greater obligation to plan lessons for pupils who have low levels of prior attainment or come from disadvantaged backgrounds. Teachers should use appropriate assessment to set targets which are deliberately ambitious. (Department for Education, 2014, p. 8)

The National Curriculum was accompanied by policy that laid responsibility for mapping and ensuring progression with schools and dramatically influenced the ways in which many teachers and schools use assessment. At classroom level, teachers generally incorporate AfL as the main purpose for using assessment, but they are also now required to report on achievement and progress for each year group. As explained in Chapter 2, the *Commission on Assessment Without Levels* has been established with the remit to support schools in introducing target and accountability systems to ensure all learners are on track and all reach agreed standards.

In many schools, separate systems exist for tracking achievement and progress from those used for assessing and responding on a daily basis through AfL. Running two concurrent systems results in greater teacher workload and sometimes an incoherence in the messages that teachers give to students (and their parents) about how children are doing. As yet, the full consequences of these two UK government decisions are not known, but they have certainly affected the ways in which teachers are asked to report to both senior leaders in schools and to parents, with a greater focus on age-expected performance rather than on learning.

A Focus on the Disciplines

From the early days of implementation of AfL, we have known that that this approach has both generic features that will apply to all stages of schooling and all subject areas, and some features that are specific to particular subjects or to students of different ages. Indeed, the KMOFAP project (Black et al., 2003) focused first on science, mathematics, and English teaching. Booklets on AfL practice for specific disciplines were subsequently produced, including science, mathematics, English, modern foreign languages, information and communication technology, geography, and design and technology.

In 2011, US assessment expert Randy Bennett published a critique of formative assessment in which he called for a focus on conceptualizing well-specified approaches built around process and methodology rooted within specific subject areas. Bennett was contesting the idea of AfL as a set of generic strategies and instead was arguing that AfL practices are shaped and bound by the discipline in which they take place. *Inside the Black Box* did not ignore the impact of specific disciplines on AfL practices, noting that it was necessary to carry out development of practice in a range of subject areas because research differs among subjects such as mathematics, science, and creative arts. However, in the US, Bennett's paper raised anew the disciplinary nature of AfL, and others have taken up the call. For instance, a newly published *Handbook of Formative Assessment in the Disciplines*, coedited by Andrade, Bennett, and Cizek (2019), focuses on the implementation of AfL practices in the context of specific disciplines, and Shepard, Penuel, and Pellegrino (2018) advocate that curriculum, instruction, and assessment must be grounded in the discipline-specific ways that core ideas and practices are developed over time.

What does this emphasis on AfL in the disciplines mean from a teacher-planning perspective? First and foremost, it highlights that teachers need to have deep disciplinary knowledge, including knowledge of the overarching concepts, themes and frameworks, forms of information representation, as well as different types of texts and the discourse practices of the discipline (Goldman et al., 2016). While these elements are found across disciplines, there are differences according to specific disciplines. For instance, when students are learning about history, they engage in a process of investigation, constructing interpretations of historical events through reading primary and secondary sources, whereas in science they generate and test explanation for phenomena through investigations in which they collect and analyze data (National Academies of Science, Engineering and Medicine, 2018).

Second, teachers need to have an understanding of how learning progresses in a discipline so that when they plan learning goals and success criteria, they place them in a larger trajectory of learning, connecting current learning to previous and future learning. By doing so they avoid the pitfalls of discrete, atomistic learning goals that the CCRS and NGSS (for example) are intended to move away from. Additionally, when teachers understand the connections and progression of topics within the discipline, they are better able to respond in ways that move learning forward from its current status (Heritage, 2008). For instance, when teaching multiplication, knowing that a progression begins with repeated addition of objects arranged in rectangular arrays, then moves to understanding the symbolic representation $(2 + 2 + 2 + 2)$ with the concrete representation (four groups of two objects) and progresses to understanding repeated addition $(2 + 2 + 2 + 2)$ as the number 2 added four times, and finally 4×2 can benefit both planning and responding to evidence as it emerges.

> *Teachers need to have an understanding of how learning progresses in a discipline so that when they plan learning goals and success criteria, they place them in a larger trajectory of learning, connecting current learning to previous and future learning.*

And third, teachers need knowledge of the growth and development of students' thinking about important ideas in the discipline (Bransford, Brown, & Cocking, 2000). When they understand the development of learning in the specific discipline, they are able to anticipate and recognize student errors, justifications, and misconceptions and to orchestrate appropriate and immediate actions intended to advance learning (Heritage & Wylie, 2019). For instance, teachers will be better positioned to recognize the error and take appropriate pedagogical action if they understand that students, in their development of proportional reasoning, may incorrectly assume additive relationships to compare ratios and assume that 2:3 is equivalent to 3:4

> *Teachers need knowledge of the growth and development of students' thinking about important ideas in the discipline.*

(Arieli-Attali, Wylie, & Bauer, 2012). Similarly, if teachers understand that students may have naïve ideas about properties of matter based on their experiences of the world—for example, associating gases with the use and function of objects such as footballs and tires—they are more equipped to address these ideas in their teaching and to attend to them should they arise.

Professional Learning for AfL

In preservice courses, candidate teachers are advised to use research to inform practice, but changing classroom practice in response to research ideas is not always an easy task. Gert Biesta, professor of education at Brunel University in the UK, argues that educational research can inform, not direct, teaching: "Research cannot supply us with rules for action but only hypotheses for intelligent problem solving" (Biesta, 2007, p. 17). If this is the case, then it follows that teachers need time to interpret and decide what and how research evidence might inform their practice. Recognizing that AfL is not another "magic bullet" for education, Black and Wiliam in *Inside the Black Box* suggested teachers would need to find answers to many of the practical questions that evidence alone could not satisfy. They should work out their own ways of incorporating AfL into their own patterns of classroom work within their specific disciplines. Changes in practice require teachers to alter the ways they work and interact with their students, which can seem both risky and challenging. The work we have both done with teachers suggests that incorporating AfL should be done slowly and pursued over time, which is sometimes tricky for teachers when they first start and are eager to try new ideas. Many teachers have told us that one of the main factors for successful change is to share experiences with a colleague, as this can provide both practical and emotional support during the change process.

Teacher Learning Communities

One mechanism that has supported teachers in figuring out AfL for themselves is participation in a teacher learning community (TLC; Wiliam & Thompson, 2008). TLCs are based on the idea of communities of practice. Put simply, communities of practice refer to groups of people who genuinely care about the same real-life problems and who interact regularly to learn together and from each other and solve problems (Wenger, McDermott, & Snyder, 2002). This is exactly what teachers aim to do in TLCs, which have become the "new paradigm" in the US, in particular to support teacher learning (Shepard, 2019).

To provide some context: Ideas about organizational management and professional learning that focus less on hierarchical structures and more on team learning (e.g., Senge, 1998) have coincided with the demands for the achievement of higher standards that we have previously discussed. Acknowledging this situation, Resnick and Hall (1998) called for learning communities to provide opportunities for common meeting times, classroom visitations, and frequent collegial conversations about student learning. In a review of the literature on effective professional learning, three main ideas emerged: It is sustained, job-embedded, and collaborative (Darling-Hammond & Richardson, 2009). No doubt in response to these ideas, the Standards for Professional Learning (Learning Forward, 2011) are emphatic that the purpose of professional learning is to assist teachers in developing the knowledge, skills, and practices they need to be effective in their classrooms, emphasizing the importance of educators taking an active role in their continuous development. In this regard, the Standards for Professional Learning specifically call out learning communities, noting that professional learning that increases educator effectiveness and results for all students occurs within learning communities committed to continuous improvement, collective responsibility, and goal alignment. The "Learning Communities" standard describes them as contexts for continuous improvement in which teachers engage in inquiry, action research, reflection, and evaluation. Learning communities foster collective participation and peer-to-peer support.

As a consequence of this rethinking about professional learning, TLCs have taken hold and have become a prominent means for teachers' inquiry about their practice. As the National Council of Teachers of English (NCTE) noted,

> As opposed to individual professional learning experiences, communities of practice open space for identifying shared practical, pedagogical, and disciplinary knowledge that might otherwise remain tacit. (2011, p. 2)

In this space, teachers work together to develop their AfL practices—for example, developing learning goals and success criteria, improving questioning strategies, examining evidence and thinking about appropriate pedagogical responses, creating lessons together, reviewing how the lesson went, considering revisions that students made to their work in order to gauge the effectiveness of their feedback, and so on.

Experience suggests that becoming effective in AfL takes time and commitment. In large part, this is because implementing AfL means changing the way teachers "think about teaching and their view of their role as a teacher" (Black et al., 2003, p. 80). While teachers may learn the "basics" of AfL from a workshop or a one-shot professional development session, these opportunities do not give them the chance to really think about their practice and the changes that are needed for effective AfL implementation. Changing practice can be a scary prospect, so the more it is done in collaboration with others, the better. Working with peers in a learning community to engage in a cycle of learn-practice-reflect-revise (Wiliam & Thompson, 2008) can provide the necessary support for continued professional learning about AfL.

In a well-structured TLC, teachers plan and prepare for changes in their classroom and share recent practice, reflect on that practice, and solicit feedback from peers. Sometimes, it is through sharing the new ways of working with like-minded peers that teachers begin to recognize, unpack, and understand the change process that they are involved in. Such discussions involve reflecting on and articulating what they did in class, why they made the choices they did, and what the responses from their students were. Developing a shared understanding of practice is useful from both an evaluative and an emotional perspective, as it can provide a common purpose for those teachers involved, which helps them be resilient if either the new classroom changes require a few attempts to implement or if students or other stakeholders are initially resistant to change. By fostering professional learning, a TLC enables teachers to take control of their own learning journey, giving legitimacy to their new practice from the professional community actions of the group (Harrison, 2013). Teachers can then, if needed, revise their implementation plans and continue to practice outside of the meeting time. An effective approach to AfL implementation is providing ongoing learning opportunities with time to put learning into practice, followed by more reflection and, if necessary, revision to practice (Wylie & Heritage, 2010).

> Developing a shared understanding of practice is useful from both an evaluative and an emotional perspective, as it can provide a common purpose for those teachers involved, which helps them be resilient if either the new classroom changes require a few attempts to implement or if students or other stakeholders are initially resistant to change.

Skilled teachers never stop learning. A case in point is two teachers from the University of California, Los Angeles, Lab School, who recently observed that, while they have been focusing on AfL for over fifteen years, they still need to work together to refine their practice. For example, they routinely share learning goals and success criteria with each other, because "*they are not always one hundred percent right.*"

One of the UK KMOFAP teachers, Paul Spenceley, recently said at a celebration of twenty years of *Inside the Black Box,*

AfL changed my teaching absolutely beyond belief. What I learned from the project was that it wasn't about how well I was teaching, it was how my students were learning. It wasn't about what students were taught, it was about learning. . . . The discussion is really important and the part that needs planning for carefully. I have never ever done more work for AfL; I have just done it differently. If a student doesn't know what success and what learning look like, both success in the short and long term, they are not going to be able to buy into it.

Concluding Thoughts

We know that good teaching and learning are built on the interactions and relationships that happen in classrooms and that what AfL does is provide the evidence and processes for teaching to work well. There are no recipes to ensure that a particular way of teaching results in effective learning, but the responsive nature of AfL and its immediacy in the classroom allow teachers to mediate and adapt teaching to support learners in developing understanding and making progress. The professional "know-how" in order to do this takes time to develop because teachers have to work out routines and practices that foster classroom climates where formative opportunities are made possible. They then have to carefully plan the challenging learning experiences that enable students to think, share, and develop their ideas because classes and students have their own experiences and needs.

In the UK, professional learning for AfL has focused strongly on a dialogic teaching approach and the development of high-order questions so that adaptation of activities is generally achieved through small- and whole-group talk. While attention has been paid to lesson objectives and success criteria, there is still some way to go to get such practices functioning well (particularly in secondary schools), where sometimes curriculum demands swamp learning needs. Part of this problem has been insufficient focus on subject disciplines and the different ways AfL fits in with particular approaches to teaching and learning in specific subject areas. So while teachers have access to some support materials through books, online resources, and through teacher organizations, there is a need to build on this support over the next few years.

In the US, the focus has been more holistic in terms of planning for learning and on helping teachers conceptualize AfL as a classroom process rather than an event or task. Such an approach has led naturally to the setting up of TLCs where professional support and challenge help teachers shape and scope their AfL practices. There has also been a drive to relate AfL to greater student agency and the role of self-regulation in learning, and while that has been explored through self- and peer assessment in the UK, the US version draws on these ideas more to explain how and why AfL works effectively in classrooms.

What we do know in both countries is that teachers have to tackle the ways they work in the classroom and evolve how AfL plays out in their setting with their students. This means teachers being both vigilant and flexible in their approach; what works with one class may not work with another. Starting with small purposeful changes as teachers strengthen their AfL practice can dramatically change how classrooms work and how learners learn to learn. The versatility, creativeness, and repertoires of some of the teachers we have had the pleasure of working with have been astounding and regularly convince us that AfL exerts a powerful influence on teaching and learning.

In the next chapter, we go more deeply into the transformations that teachers make to their classroom practice to fully incorporate AfL into their everyday work.

REFERENCES

Andrade, H., Bennett, R. E, & Cizek, G. (2019). *Handbook of formative assessment in the disciplines*. New York, NY: Routledge.

Arieli-Attali, M., Wylie, E. C., & Bauer, M. I. (2012, April). *The use of three learning progressions in supporting formative assessment in middle school mathematics*. Paper presented at the annual meeting of the American Educational Research Association, Vancouver, Canada.

Bennett, R. E. (2011). Formative assessment: A critical review. *Assessment in Education: Principles, Policy & Practice, 18*(1), 5–25.

Biesta, G. (2007). Why "what works" won't work: Evidence based practice and the democratic deficit in educational research. *Educational Theory, 57*(1), 1–22.

Black, P., & Wiliam, D. (1998a). Assessment and classroom learning. *Assessment in Education: Principles, Policy & Practice, 5*(1), 7–73.

Black, P., & Wiliam, D. (1998b). *Inside the black box: Raising standards through classroom assessment*. London, UK: School of Education, King's College London.

Black, P., Harrison, C., Lee, C., Marshall, B., & Wiliam, D. (2003). *Assessment for learning*. Berkshire, UK: Open University Press.

Black, P., Wilson M., & Yao, S-Y. (2011). Roadmaps for learning: A guide to the navigation of learning progressions. *Measurement: Interdisciplinary Research and Perspectives, 9*(2–3), 71–123.

Bransford, J., Brown, A. L., & Cocking, R. R. (2000). *How people learn: Brain, mind, experience, and school.* Commission on Behavioral and Social Sciences and Education National Research Council. Washington, DC: National Academy Press.

Bunch, G. C., Kibler, A., & Pimental, A. (2012). Realizing opportunities for English learners in the common core English language arts and disciplinary literacy standards. In K. Hakuta & M. Santos (Eds.), *Understanding language: Commissioned papers on language and literacy issues in the Common Core State Standards and Next Generation Science Standards* (pp. 1–16). Palo Alto, CA: Stanford University.

Darling-Hammond, L., & Richardson, N. (2009). Teacher learning: What matters? *Educational Leadership, 66*(5), 46–53.

Department for Education. (2014). *National curriculum in England framework document.* London, UK: HMSO.

Goldman, S. R., Britt, M. A., Brown, W., Cribb, G., George, M., Greenleaf, C., . . . Project READI. (2016). Disciplinary literacies and learning to read for understanding: A conceptual framework for disciplinary literacy. *Educational Psychologist, 51*(2), 219–246.

Harrison, C. (2013) Collaborative action research as a tool for generating formative feedback on teachers' classroom assessment practice: The KREST project. *Teachers and Teaching: Theory and Practice (19)*2, 202–213.

Heritage, M. (2008). *Learning progressions: Supporting instruction and formative assessment.* Washington, DC: Council of Chief State School Officers.

Heritage, M. (2010). *Formative assessment: Making it happen in the classroom.* Thousand Oaks, CA: Corwin.

Heritage, M., & Wylie, E. C. (2019). Teacher preparation in mathematics. In H. L. Andrade, R. E. Bennett, & G. J. Cizek (Eds.), *Handbook of formative assessment in the disciplines* (pp. 207–243). New York: NY: Routledge.

Lampert, M., Loef Franke, M., Kazemi, E., Ghousseini, H., Chan Turrou, A., Beasley, H., . . . Crowe, K. (2013). Keeping it complex: Using rehearsals to support novice teacher learning of ambitious teaching. *Journal of Teacher Education, 64*, 226–243.

Learning Forward. (2011). *Standards for professional learning: Learning communities.* Oxford, OH: Learning Forward.

Lee, O., Quinn, H., & Valdés, G. (2013). Science and language for English language learners in relation to Next Generation Science Standards and with implications for Common Core State Standards for English language arts and mathematics. *Educational Researcher, 42*(4), 223–233.

Moschkovich, J. (2012). Mathematics, the common core and language: Recommendations for mathematics instruction for ELLs aligned with the common core. In K. Hakuta & M. Santos (Eds.), *Understanding language: Commissioned papers on language and literacy issues in the Common Core State Standards and Next Generation Science Standards* (pp. 17–31). Palo Alto, CA: Stanford University.

National Academies of Sciences, Engineering and Medicine. (2018). *How people learn II: Learners, context, and cultures*. Washington, DC: National Academies Press.

National Council of Teachers of English. (2011). *Communities of practice: A policy research brief*. Urbana, IL: NCTE.

National Council of Teachers of Mathematics. (2014). *Principles into actions: Ensuring mathematical success for all*. Reston, VA: NCTM.

Resnick, L. B., & Hall, M. W. (1998). Learning organizations for sustainable education reform. *Daedalus, 127*(4), 89–118.

Senge, P. (1998). Sharing knowledge: You can't own knowledge, so why not share it? *Executive Excellence, 15*, 11–12.

Shepard, L. A. (2019). Classroom assessment to support teaching and learning. In A. Berman, M. J. Feuer, & J. W. Pellegrino (Eds.), *The Annals of the American Academy of Political and Social Science* (pp. 183–200). Thousand Oaks, CA: SAGE.

Shepard, L. A., Penuel, W. R., & Pellegrino, J. W. (2018). Using learning and motivation theories to coherently link formative assessment, grading practices, and large scale assessment. *Educational Measurement: Issues and Practice, 37*(1), 21–34.

Stiggins, R. (2007). Conquering the formative assessment frontier. In J. McMillan (Ed.), *Formative classroom assessment: Theory into practice* (pp. 8–28). New York, NY: Teachers College Press.

Swaffield, S. (2011). Getting to the heart of authentic assessment for learning. *Assessment in Education, 18*(4), 433–449.

Teaching Channel. (n.d.) *Transcript for lesson, conjecturing about functions*. Retrieved from https://www.teachingchannel.org/videos/conjecturelessonplan

Wenger, E., McDermott, R. A., & Snyder, W. (2002). *Cultivating communities of practice: A guide to managing knowledge*. Cambridge, MA: Harvard Business Press.

Wiliam, D., & Thompson, M. (2008). Integrating assessment with learning: What will make it work. In C. A. Dwyer (Ed.), *The future of assessment: Shaping teaching and learning* (pp. 53–82). Mahwah, NJ: Lawrence Erlbaum Associates.

Windschitl, M. (2002). Framing constructivism in practice as the negotiation of dilemmas: An analysis of the conceptual, pedagogical, cultural, and political challenges facing teachers. *Review of Educational Research, 72*(2), 131–175.

Windschitl, M., Thompson, J., & Braaten, M. (2011). Ambitious pedagogy by novice teachers: Who benefits from tool-supported collaborative inquiry into practice and why? *Teachers College Record, 113*(7), 1311–1360.

Wylie, E. C., & Heritage, M. (2010). Developing and deepening formative assessment practice. In M. Heritage (Ed.), *Formative assessment: Making it happen in the classroom* (pp. 117–131). Thousand Oaks, CA: Corwin.

Transforming Classrooms

Assessment for learning (AfL) can be distinguished from other forms of assessment by its purpose: to enhance learning rather than to measure learning (Cowie, 2005). In *Inside the Black Box*, Black and Wiliam (1998) made clear that to achieve this purpose, AfL had to be embedded into classroom practice, and successfully embedding AfL required changes in how teachers do business in their classrooms:

> *It is hard to see how any innovation in formative assessment (AfL) can be treated as a marginal change in classroom work. All such work involves some degree of feedback between those taught and the teacher, and this is entailed in the quality of their interactions, which is at the heart of pedagogy.* (Black & Wiliam, 1998, p. 16)

In a single sentence, the foundations of AfL were established. The implications from this sentence for classroom practice are as follows:

1. The changes in classroom routines and practices are likely to be major.

2. All activities require feedback between the students and the teacher.

3. The classroom dialogue and interchanges of ideas need to be rich.

In this chapter, we explore why implementing AfL cannot be a marginal change in classroom work, how teachers can bring about the necessary changes to incorporate feedback loops between them and their students into their practice, and how they can make interaction the heart of pedagogy.

We begin with a reflection by Shawn, a secondary school teacher, on the changes that occurred in his classroom as a result of implementing AfL (the underlining is his):

> *I used to do a lot of <u>explaining</u>, but now I do a lot of questioning.*
>
> *I used to do a lot of <u>talking</u>, but now I do a lot of <u>listening</u>.*
>
> *I used to think about teaching the <u>curriculum</u>, but now I think about teaching the <u>student</u>.* (Heritage, 2010, p. 4)

From Shawn's reflection, it is possible to imagine the kind of changes he made to his practice, and they are certainly not marginal. He now obtains evidence from questioning and listening to students' responses and discussions, and he uses the evidence to advance the learning of each student. It is as though he has turned 180 degrees in his classroom practice to enable AfL to be fully embedded in teaching and learning.

Making the kinds of transformations that Shawn described are not a simple fix. One catalyst advocated by Black and Wiliam to set these transformations into motion is for teachers to engage in "scrutiny" of the teaching plan. This scrutiny needs to be undergirded by a belief that the transmission model of learning is **not** the most effective one and by a commitment to teach through interaction—the heart of pedagogy. The scrutiny includes a consideration of the nature of learning tasks, of classroom questioning and discussions, and of opportunities for students to explain their thinking. In this vein, we can recognize the shift that Shawn has made; his focus is now on listening and responding to students rather than on his own predetermined teaching.

Transforming practice comes slowly after teachers make a commitment to AfL and invest in improving their AfL practice over time. In the next section, we'll look more closely at what transforming practice entails.

Transforming Practice

The difficulties of teachers making changes to their practice are well documented (e.g., Hargreaves & Fullan, 2012). Teachers tend to be pragmatic with a keen eye for specific, practical ideas that directly relate to the day-to-day operation of their classrooms (Fullan & Miles, 1992). However, introducing AfL into their practice means that teachers cannot simply add new strategies and ideas into what they already do in an attempt to make space for them within their current teaching repertoire. Instead, for many teachers, embedding AfL into teaching and learning really does require a transformation of practice. This is because AfL necessitates teachers taking a more responsive approach to learning and incorporating both student ideas and opportunities for them to develop self-regulatory processes—for example, goal setting, assessing their own learning, and making decisions about next steps.

Transformation does not happen overnight. Teachers do not move from zero to perfection in one move. Instead, they need to gradually make changes to their current practice to allow new ways of working to filter into the classroom practices and routines and gradually merge into their everyday teaching repertoire. Doing this is not always easy. But as a teacher who had become expert in AfL said when asked what advice she would give to peers who were starting their journey, "*Don't give up when it gets hard—you'll find it's worth it.*"

As an illustration of the kind of transformations needed in practice, let us examine the ideas of the "spirit" and the "letter" of AfL.

The Spirit and the Letter of AfL

Two UK researchers, Bethan Marshall and Mary Jane Drummond (2006), coined the terms *spirit* and the *letter* of AfL to capture the idea of teacher practice that adopted surface procedures of AfL ("letter") and practice that incorporated the deeper principles of AfL ("spirit"). As a component of their research study on AfL practice, they videoed two teachers of English (English language arts) who were teaching separate eighth-grade classes (13-year-olds). Both teachers were attempting to do similar things in similar contexts. In the two lessons, the teachers used elements central to AfL: They shared the assessment criteria with their students by giving them a model of what was expected. The students then used the criteria to assess the work of their peers.

In Lesson A, students looked at a letter based on a Victorian short story. The teacher modeled the criteria by giving the students an example of a letter that was full of errors. The students were asked to make the corrections on their own. The teacher then went through the corrections with the whole class before asking the students to read and correct the work of their peers.

In Lesson B, students were asked to consider a dramatic rendition of a 19th-century poem. The teacher and the classroom assistant performed the poem to the class and invited the students to critique their performance. From this activity, the class as a whole, assisted by the teacher, established criteria for performing a poem. These criteria then guided both the students' thinking about what was needed when they acted out the poem themselves and the peer assessment of those performances that followed. This teacher's goal was for her students to understand the quality of the work rather than focusing on what was or was not included in the performance or what was correct or incorrect.

The difference between these two lessons lies in the ways the teachers framed and actioned peer assessment. Lesson A was an example of an AfL activity being followed to the "letter" because students were only being challenged to meet the teacher's expectations. The teacher wanted her students to know how she assessed their work and whether they could identify the same mistakes that she noticed. By contrast, in Lesson B the teacher wanted students to develop an idea of what quality in a task looked like in advance of engaging in the task themselves. After they established the criteria for quality and saw it in action, students were more prepared to make judgments about

> *To embed AfL effectively in their classroom practice, teachers have to acquire the "spirit" of AfL rather than operating to the "letter."*

their peers' work and also to reflect in a more nuanced way on their own performance. Lesson B fits with the "spirit" of AfL because the sequence of activities helped students both to think and to learn how to learn for themselves. To embed AfL effectively in their classroom practice, teachers have to acquire the "spirit" of AfL rather than operating to the "letter." We'll move now to consider what is entailed in making the necessary transformations in practice that permit the "spirit" of AfL to be embedded in the daily work of teachers and students.

AfL Pedagogy

The vast majority of teachers seek evidence of how students are doing and give them advice on how they could do better. Often, teachers believe this task is best accomplished through tests and quizzes and by marking and grading work. The inferences that teachers make from data collected by these methods is restricted in the ways it can influence future teaching and learning. For example, in general, quizzes provide quick audits of knowledge and tend to be limited to checks on terminology, simple calculations, or brief factual information. Quizzes might check if a student knows the date of an important historical event but do not tell the teacher whether the students understand the significance of that event within its historical context. Tests or examinations may have the capacity to examine more aspects of student thinking and understanding than quizzes can, but the process of marking delays any action based on this evidence, plus the emotional investment involved with testing limits its use in supporting learning.

Students (and many teachers) do not regard tests as providing information on where they need to focus their near-future efforts. And they are mostly right. Frequently, tests focus on whether students can do a predetermined thing and provide information about correct and incorrect responses (Torrance & Pryor, 1998). They do not provide the "qualitative insights" (Shepard, 2005) that are needed in AfL. As a result, students are informed that they achieved a certain grade, mark, or percentage rather than having descriptive feedback about areas for improvement. So students might tell their parents that they got 76 percent on their history test rather than that they did well and now need "to be clear about the significance and influences of different causes rather than simply listing and explaining them." Also, while teachers might make mental notes of areas of learning that need further attention after a test, typically the main action they take is to record the mark as evidence to inform reports and later decisions about students. Here, the purpose is more for accountability than for formative action.

How teachers view assessment goes hand-in-hand with the pedagogical approach that they adopt as a result of their view about how students learn. Most teachers think of themselves as practitioners rather than theoreticians, but nearly all teachers' practice is guided by theory, whether consciously or not (Heritage, Walqui, & Linquanti, 2015). We can clearly see the theories that guided how Shawn taught before incorporating AfL into his practice. He had moved from a transmission view of learning to one that centered on the sense students were making of their learning. Along the same lines, in *Inside the Black Box*, Black and Wiliam (1998) noted that when teachers accept the wealth of evidence that this transmission model does not work, even when judged by its own criteria, they are willing to make a commitment to teaching through interaction.

When teachers adopt a transmission theory of learning, assessment becomes the means to find out if the learning was transmitted correctly. Is the student's response right or wrong? With a theory of learning that embraces interaction at its heart, students' thinking and the development of ideas are central, and teachers are concerned to understand that thinking while students are in the process of learning. The difference between the two approaches is summed up by these scholars: "What ultimately counts is the extent to which instruction requires students to think, not just to report someone else's thinking" (Nystrand, Gamoran, Kachur, & Prendergast, 1997, p. 72).

Let's now look more closely at how teachers develop AfL practices and the journey they undertake.

Developing AfL Practices

In the AfL approach, learning is both process-driven and progressive, relying not only on teacher planning but also on how students respond to activities, to questions during the lesson, and to one another. Assessment and guidance are in action throughout the lesson, not just at set points. While the

> *Making major changes does not necessarily mean that teachers need to learn afresh how to teach. Instead, they need to their use existing skills and knowledge differently for a new purpose.*

focus of each lesson part may have a different function, the intention of AfL is to provide continuous feedback throughout the lesson for both the teacher and the students. As we noted at the beginning of this chapter, major changes in practice are likely to be needed to include AfL as an integral part of teaching and learning.

Making major changes does not necessarily mean that teachers need to learn afresh how to teach. Instead, they need to use their existing skills and knowledge differently for a new purpose.

They may well have to refine these skills, however—for example, moving from listening to student responses to listening for how students respond in classroom interactions (Mason, 2017), which, of course, is consistent with an approach to teaching that centers on developing student thinking.

Taking the First Steps

Teachers want to do the best for their students, so when introduced to research suggesting that a particular type of classroom assessment will raise achievement, they are usually keen to try this assessment approach in their classrooms. When teachers first try out AfL, many think that some strategies needed for implementation fit easily into their existing practice and make sense in terms of refining their current practice. For example, increasing the "wait time" (Rowe, 1976) between asking a question and receiving an answer provides more time for student thought and recollection and is likely to result in fuller and richer responses. Such changes in practice do not require detailed and time-consuming preparation, nor do they interfere a great deal with what normally happens in lessons, so teachers view this AfL strategy as feasible and believe it has potential.

Similarly, teachers see the use of self-assessment strategies—such as "Traffic Lighting," where students simply place either a green, amber, or red dot on a piece of work to indicate their confidence in completing the work successfully—as easily fitting in to current practice. When reviewing the colored dots, the teacher is alerted to whether there is general understanding across the class or if students may need more support in a future lesson. This simple feedback mechanism is easily incorporated into everyday practice, so teachers feel that they can manage this change.

The problem with adopting such strategies as Traffic Lighting is that they simply increase the input evidence. Furthermore, in the case of Traffic Lighting, without exploring students' decisions to signal their work by a color, the quality of the input is very limited. This concern also applies to other strategies, such as increasing wait time (Rowe, 1976). While teachers may give increased wait time for students to respond to their questions, if the questions are not designed to generate substantive responses from students, the evidence will also be limited. Generating quality evidence that provides insights into learning requires thought and planning, and we will return to this idea later in the chapter.

However, obtaining quality evidence is only a first step. What teachers decide to do in response to the evidence is the key to learning and improvement. Only when teachers use the classroom evidence to make decisions about next steps in learning and then continually oversee what is happening as students revisit and reconsider their ideas are learning gains made. While simple changes such as wait time or Traffic Lighting may signal formative intentions, improving student learning requires considered formative action in response to evidence. As they start trying out AfL in their classrooms, teachers need to be reflecting on the changes they are making, asking themselves "*What evidence of learning am I getting from the changes I am making?*" and "*How are my responses helping this student's learning?*"

Returning to the Traffic Lighting strategy for a moment, the teacher's response to the essays with red and amber dots might be to correct mistakes or tell students to "add detail" to give them a sense of what a better essay could look like. However, this kind of response does not expose and challenge more deep-seated problems that students might be experiencing. If the students have not reopened their thinking on these areas, the feedback that the teacher has given does not form a sufficient scaffold for students to reconstruct their thinking and move to a more successful performance. Crafting and constructing feedback comments that encourage students to revisit their ideas and provide better answers to the original question or problem requires a challenging task for teachers, but one that is likely to help learners improve.

In an effort to improve the use of feedback by students, recently many schools in the UK have introduced a strategy called "Green Pen Marking." This new strategy provides time in the lesson for students to use the written feedback that the teacher has provided and, in green pen, show their response to the feedback. The important part here is what the feedback asks students to do. In many cases, feedback simply requires students to add examples or use specific terminology; such actions alert students to teacher expectations but rarely encourage them to reflect on aspects of quality in the assessed piece. In contrast, Green Pen Marking could reengage the students with the learning and help them reflect more deeply on their current and developing understanding.

Strengthening Classroom Talk and Questioning

When introducing AfL, teachers routinely work on a range of strategies that strengthen classroom talk both to prompt learners into becoming more active in discussion and to improve how they probe student thinking. When teachers take steps to strengthen classroom talk, the result is that more students volunteer to answer and elaborate on their answers than previously, which, in turn, leads to students responding and interacting with one another with increasing confidence. In some classrooms, the change in classroom talk is huge, moving from single-word answers from a handful of students to a purposeful discussion driven by student ideas (Black et al., 2003). This change was evident in Sarah's classroom in the vignette in Chapter 1 when she gradually coached her student to become more active in discussion, while at the same time working on how she could develop more probing questions to stimulate student thinking and talk. In classrooms that generate rich discussion, teachers are able to select which of the many diverse student ideas and experiences are productive starting points for navigating between everyday forms of knowing and those accepted and used within specific content areas (Bang & Medin, 2010).

Teachers also often work on strengthening their questioning skills through finding or constructing questions that encourage student thinking. In some cases, a good question can stimulate a discussion that becomes an activity in itself, while in others a question can help students fully engage with an activity so that they achieve more productive outcomes. To illustrate: In one lesson, Paul, a high school science teacher, changed his usual question "How is the cactus adapted to desert conditions?" to "If plants need sunlight to grow, then why don't we find the largest plants in the desert?" This change of approach in questioning engaged the students much more. They realized that their teacher was not asking them to recall facts and build an explanation as he had done previously, but instead was asking them to engage in problem-solving. As we have seen previously, the use of the pronoun we suggested he wanted to co-construct knowledge and signaled to the students that he wanted to discuss and share ideas to eventually reach a solution. In other words, what Paul achieved was far more than finding a better question to assess understanding of adaptation: He had skillfully changed the power balance and classroom expectations to nudge learning forward.

To assist in improving their questioning skills, some teachers turn to Benjamin Bloom's (1956) taxonomy of questions, a hierarchical framework of cognitive skills that is often used to evaluate educational goals. The original sequence of cognitive skills in Bloom's taxonomy was (from lowest to highest) knowledge, comprehension, application, analysis, synthesis, and evaluation. Bloom's framework was revised by Lorin Anderson and David Krathwohl and associates (2001) and titled A Taxonomy for Teaching, Learning, and Assessment, drawing attention away from the somewhat static notion of educational objectives to suggest a more dynamic conception of the classification.

Anderson and Krathwohl et al. replaced comprehension from Bloom's taxonomy with understanding and synthesis with creativity. Their definition of understanding began with making meaning from instructional messages of various forms and included the skills of summarizing, classifying, and predicting, which went beyond Bloom's comprehension definition of locating and extracting relevant information. They introduced creativity as the highest level of their revised taxonomy, which includes the ability to design, construct, and generate novel ideas. When students are making meaning and being creative, they are involved in taking actions and producing something that illustrates their capabilities in these cognitive areas. The richer view of learning goals proposed in Anderson et al.'s taxonomy supports selecting or designing relevant classroom activities that result in a more actionable interpretation than Bloom encouraged. Anderson et al. also mapped the six levels of cognitive skills across the types of knowledge that students might engage with as they progressed from simple concrete knowledge through procedural and conceptual understanding toward metacognition and the ability to manipulate increasingly abstract ideas. Here is an example of how one teacher, Janice, used the revised taxonomy to encourage thinking and discussion in a technology/art class for 10-year-olds, in which the students had made board games and practiced playing the games according to the "maker's rules."

- *Can you explain the aim of the game in one sentence?* (Understanding)

- *Which rules were easy, and which were difficult to follow?* (Understanding)

- *Which rules would you need to change if you had extra players to include in the game?* (Analysis and Application)

- *How could you adapt the game so that you could recognize the winner much more quickly?* (Creativity)

Questioning to Prompt Thinking

Initially during the King's–Medway–Oxfordshire Formative Assessment Project (KMOFAP) discussed in previous chapters, some of the participating teachers tried using Bloom's taxonomy to improve their questioning skills. However, several of them found this system challenging to use on a regular basis in their classrooms. To overcome this difficulty, mathematics teachers evolved a new approach, devising question stems to construct a range of questions for a topic, which teachers could select from to use in their lessons. Some of the question stems were as follows:

- *How can we be sure that _____?*
- *Why is _____ an example of _____?*
- *What is the same and what is different about _____?*
- *Is it ever/always true/false that _____?*
- *Why do _____, _____, and _____ all give the same answer?*
- *How do you _____?*
- *How would you explain _____?*
- *What does that tell us about _____?*
- *What is wrong with _____?*
- *Why is _____ true?*

This approach was trialed first with lessons on ratios with 12-year-old students. Questions the teachers used in this context included the following:

- *What's similar and what's different about ratios and fractions?*
- *Is it always true in ratios that the first number is larger than the second?*
- *Why do 12:9, 15:5, and 6:2 all give the same answer?*

- *How do you explain a ratio of 5:4 for a group in which there are fewer boys than girls?*

- *How would you explain a ratio of 3:2 in terms of butter and sugar in a recipe?*

- *What is "wrong" with a ratio of 5.5:3.3?*

Partway through the topic on ratios, one teacher started a lesson by asking, *"What's similar and different about ratios and fractions?"* This created a lively discussion around students' ideas of *"ratios being like sideways fractions"* and *"the importance of division"* and *"understanding the size of the parts and the whole"* and why *"the 1 in a 3:1 ratio was not a third."* It was evident in this classroom discussion that the mathematical thinking went beyond the procedural to a higher conceptual level. After the class discussion, while the rest of the class started an assignment on ratios, a few pairs of students continued the conversation. This was a good example of students evaluating their own understanding though discussing with peers, rather than quietly working individually through an assignment of ratio questions in their mathematics class.

The KMOFAP mathematics teachers not only found this approach to developing good questions successful, but they quickly came to realize that these question stems were applicable to other topics. In a short time, teachers of other subject disciplines also began using the question stems, and while they sometimes had to adapt the wording slightly to fit with their disciplines, question stems became the dominant method for developing higher-order questions.

Dialogic Teaching

More recent professional learning in the UK on encouraging talk in the classroom has centered on dialogic teaching. Many studies have mapped the type of talk that happens in classrooms (e.g., Scott, Mortimer, & Aguiar, 2006), and from these studies, it is clear that in the majority of classrooms the teacher is responsible for most of what is said. Over a three-year period, the KMOFAP project explored how science, mathematics, and English (ELA) secondary school teachers generally started their lessons and found that teachers typically began lessons with question-and-answer sessions intended to link the current lesson with previous learning experiences (Black et al., 2003). At the start of the KMOFAP project, teacher talk dominated in most of the lesson starters by an average word count of 10:1. While teachers did try to engage learners by asking questions, the required answers tended to be limited to one-word or one-sentence responses. Beginning lessons in this way tipped the dominance of talk in favor of teacher talk and diminished opportunities for students to express their ideas. As a result, teachers had difficulty in obtaining evidence of the current status of their students' learning. Gradually, as teachers became more accomplished in AfL, they were more successful at asking effective questions that generated extended responses and illuminated students' thinking.

Deciding when to intervene and when to allow talk to continue is a vital skill in the AfL classroom. Let us return to our science lesson from Chapter 3—in which one student offered evidence on her experience with plants, reporting how she had noticed that there were no gaps around plant roots and how she regarded this as evidence that plants do not get food from the soil and so photosynthesis must be true. In this scenario, the teacher, Casey, asked the class to discuss in pairs what they thought of the evidence being offered. Most agreed with the evidence, but three pairs disagreed—two pairs because they said that photosynthesis was what leaves did and so had nothing to do with the roots; another pair disagreed because it said the roots' tightness has to do with the soil and whether it was dry or wet and not to do with the plant. Taking the initial evidence and the disagreements and using these within the class discussion allowed the teacher the opportunity to link photosynthesis with the way that plants feed and how they grow. While the teacher did not dismiss answers, she was able to steer the students to think about and make the connections between photosynthesis, nutrition, and growth.

Another important lesson from this example is that stopping student talk too soon might mean that the teacher does not fully understand a problem that students are experiencing with a particular concept, while allowing the talk to continue for too long may result in a "bird walk" where students veer off topic, or leave insufficient time in the lesson for ideas to be challenged or for problems to be addressed. Fostering classroom talk so that ideas are aired and connections are encouraged and highlighted is a skillful strategy that teachers need to develop, as this can often be the driver for developing students' understanding.

Many of the transformations teachers make to implement AfL center on the role of students in the learning and assessment process, underscoring that their role does not take a back seat to that of the teacher's. Now, we'll explore the changing role of students in AfL.

The Changing Role of Students

A secondary school mathematics teacher in the US characterized the changing roles of teachers and students in her observation, "*Formative assessment (AfL) has not only changed me as a teacher, but I believe it has also changed my students as learners.*" She also added, "*I feel like formative assessment has helped me enter a partnership with my students with regard to learning*" (Heritage, 2010, p. 5). What did she mean by the change in her students as learners and her entering into a partnership with them? And how did these changes come about?

First, to be able to access students' thinking during the course of learning, she had completely transformed her pedagogy, moving from a stand-and-deliver approach—the transmission model—in which she talked and demonstrated and students listened and practiced what she had demonstrated—to one that was inquiry-based and required students to collaborate with each other and to solve problems. This was a major change for the students, who were prompted to take an active role in their learning as opposed to the passive stance that was more typical of their school experience. Second, this teacher helped students to understand their goal for each lesson and to internalize the success criteria (often co-constructing the criteria with her students) so they understood what meeting the goal entailed. This understanding provided students with the means to monitor their own learning, to self-assess, and to provide feedback to their peers. Third, she focused on how to give feedback through her own modeling of feedback to students and other techniques, such as a fishbowl—when students listened to pairs of peers offering feedback to each other, after which the whole class discussed the strengths and weaknesses of the feedback provided and what improvements could be made. She made sure to structure time in the classroom for self-assessment and peer feedback so that it became integral to student learning rather than a nonessential add-on, as it is sometimes viewed.

An eleventh-grade English composition teacher in the US also made similar changes in her classroom and unsurprisingly encountered several bumps along the way. For example, she found that while students were good at raising questions about writing in general, they experienced challenges in asking questions about their own writing related to the success criteria for the purpose of self-assessment. In her first attempt at peer feedback, students "graded" each other, resulting in some students being very upset because their peers gave them low grades. One student even told her she felt no one in the class was intelligent enough to provide feedback on her writing! However, this teacher did not give up—she believed the payoff for her and her students would be too great. So she persevered, guiding her students on how they could self-assess to make decisions about their own next steps and how to provide effective peer feedback. Ultimately, she was very pleased with the results, both in terms of how students were actively involved in their own learning and in the quality of writing they were producing. Read her own words:

> *This process puts the students in charge of their own writing; the level of critical thinking has improved way beyond what I used to get, and the quality of what they are turning in is so far beyond what I imagined it could be.*

Black and Wiliam suggested that the changes in classroom routines to enable AfL to take hold were likely to be significant. In the next section, we'll consider how classroom routines can impact the effectiveness of AfL.

Classroom Routines

As we noted earlier, Black and Wiliam observed in *Inside the Black Box* (1998) that interaction is at the heart of pedagogy. Getting to the heart of pedagogy demands very different classroom routines than ones that generally apply in classrooms that operate on the transmission model of learning. In such a classroom, the routines might be something like this: Students enter the classroom, take their seats, listen to and watch the teacher, perhaps taking notes, respond to a few questions, which are generally centered on guessing the answer the teacher wants, and finally complete an assignment, often to practice what the teacher has "taught" them. While that might be an ungenerous picture of a classroom, personal observation suggests it is widespread. A classroom that is centered on inquiry, discourse, questioning, deep thinking, feedback, and metacognition as advocated in *Inside the Black Box,* all of which are congruent with existing cognitive research (Black, Wilson, & Yao, 2011), requires routines to support learning. In turn, these routines make AfL possible.

We have already pointed to the importance of a classroom culture that is conducive to AfL and have emphasized such a culture as one that permits students to express ideas and reveal their thinking through interactions and responding to questions—where listening to student talk initially takes priority over correcting ideas. Such a culture involves creating a safe classroom environment in which students' ideas are valued, regardless of whether they are partially formed or just emerging (Heritage, 2013). Routines—the actions in the classroom that are regularly followed—are essential to establishing a safe environment for learning and a context in which AfL can prosper.

When teachers are working to strengthen classroom talk, students will participate in dialogue with others, within different participant structures—for example, dyads and small groups. To do this successfully, both for the purposes of learning and for AfL, all students need to understand the behavioral expectations of learning with others, including understanding routines that support collaboration and recognizing what their roles and responsibilities are to their peers to ensure quality learning for all group participants.

Routines such as listening carefully to each other, building on each other's ideas, asking questions, and finding respectful ways to disagree will all need to be established, taught, and maintained.

Routines such as listening carefully to each other, building on each other's ideas, asking questions, and finding respectful ways to disagree will all need to be established, taught, and maintained.

Similarly, routines for answering teachers' questions, such as "wait time," no interruptions when peers are talking, and no judgmental or negative comments in response to peers' answers, will provide feelings of safety for student participation. It is instructive to note that what teachers see students do may not reflect what they are capable of doing if they do not trust others to have their best interests at heart.

Asking students to think about answers to teachers' questions by either jotting down notes or talking with a peer in pairs before volunteering their answers to the whole class is another routine that can help students be more confident about talking in front of their peers. Furthermore, if a question is worth answering, then students need time to reflect on it before responding. Also, let us not forget that the central purpose of questioning in AfL is to gain insights into student thinking, so the more routines in place to support thoughtful answers, the better.

Predictable routines in the way a lesson is organized can be beneficial for AfL. For instance, the high school English teacher we encountered earlier has a predictable routine for her lessons (usually three to four class periods) that involves establishing success criteria with her students through analyzing exemplar text, independent writing, self-assessment to determine questions for peer feedback, peer feedback opportunities, and again self-assessment to decide a goal based on the feedback. Throughout this process, the teacher conferences with students, gaining insights into their learning and helping them think about their next goal. Similarly, an elementary teacher has predictable routines for her students, and because of their age, she provides many scaffolds. For example, peer feedback is a routine part of the lesson, and to support this process, she spends time teaching and practicing peer feedback with a form that structures the feedback as P (a put up—what the peer did well), Q (a clarifying question to ask), and S (suggestion for improvement).

Navigating the Landscape

In classrooms where AfL works well, an emphasis is on what the teacher does to encourage and guide students in their learning. In this regard, the role of the teacher can be thought of as guiding students across an educational landscape rather than delivering a curriculum. This idea is echoed in Shawn's comment at the start of this chapter that he now "teaches the students" rather than teaching the "curriculum." The analogy has advantages in that once teachers have become skilled guides, it is easier for them to adapt practice even if the educational landscape changes—for instance, if new curricula or standards are introduced.

As a guide rather than a transmitter of knowledge, teachers also have more scope for responding to individual needs in that the degree of scaffolding and support offered to students can be modified to match the demands of the terrain. While some routes toward the final learning goal may be familiar to the teacher—because they have trodden that path before during their own schooling and have led students along similar paths more recently—other routes may be new. As they explore new routes with their students, teachers' understanding of the landscape increases. Also, within the guiding analogy, the long-term goal for student achievement, while initially set by teacher expectations and student aspirations, can be reviewed, adapted, and reset once the journey is under way.

In summary, implementing AfL requires major changes in classrooms. Central to AfL practice is that students are actively involved and truly understand that the activities and interactions in lessons are geared toward helping them become better learners. The success of such practice builds on the relationship between the teacher and the student and is advanced through collaborative and negotiated classroom endeavor. The teacher creates the opportunities for AfL to drive learning through the activities selected and the questions and prompts that stimulate interactions. They also manage the classroom climate to foster learning and expectations of improvement, such that the students are motivated to play a meaningful role in deciding what to learn and how to learn it.

In the next and final chapter, we consider areas that still need to be explored in advancing AfL over the next twenty years.

REFERENCES

Anderson, L. W., Krathwohl, D. R., Airasian, P. W., Cruikshank, K. A., Mayer, R. E., Pintrich, P. R., & Wittrock, M. C. (2001). *A taxonomy for learning, teaching, and assessing: A revision of Bloom's taxonomy of educational objectives, abridged edition.* White Plains, NY: Longman.

Bang, M., & Medin, D. (2010). Cultural processes in science education: Supporting the navigation of multiple epistemologies. *Science Education, 94*(6), 1008–1026.

Black, P., Harrison, C., Lee, C., Marshall, B., & Wiliam, D. (2003). *Assessment for learning: Putting it into practice.* New York, NY: Open University Press.

Black, P., & Wiliam, D. (1998). Assessment and classroom learning. *Assessment in Education: Principles, Policy & Practice, 5*(1), 7–73.

Black, P., Wilson, M., & Yao, S. Y. (2011). Road maps for learning: A guide to the navigation of learning progressions. *Measurement: Interdisciplinary Research & Perspective, 9*(2–3), 71–123.

Bloom, B. S. (1956). Taxonomy of educational objectives. *Cognitive Domain,* 120–124.

Cowie, B. (2005). Pupil commentary on assessment for learning. *The Curriculum Journal, 16*(2), 137–151.

Fullan, M. G., & Miles, M. B. (1992). Getting reform right: What works and what doesn't. *Phi Delta Kappan, 73*(10), 745–752.

Hargreaves, A., & Fullan, M. (2012). *Professional capital: Transforming teaching in every school.* New York: NY: Teachers College Press.

Heritage, M. (2010). *Formative assessment: Making it happen in the classroom.* Thousand Oaks, CA: Corwin.

Heritage, M. (2013). *Formative assessment in practice: A process of inquiry and action.* Cambridge, MA: Harvard Education Press.

Heritage, M., Walqui, A., & Linquanti, R. (2015). *English language learners and the new standards: Developing language, content knowledge, and analytical practices in the classroom.* Cambridge, MA: Harvard Education Press.

Marshall, B., & Drummond, M. J. (2006). How teachers engage with assessment for learning: Lessons from the classroom. *Research Papers in Education, 21*(2), 133–149.

Mason, J. (2017). Probing beneath the surface of experience. In E. Schack, M. Fisher, & J. Wilhelm (Eds.), *Teacher noticing: Bridging and broadening perspectives, contexts, and frameworks* (pp. 1–17). New York, NY: Springer.

Nystrand, M., Gamoran, A., Kachur, R., & Prendergast, C. J. (1997). *Opening dialogue: Understanding the dynamics of language and learning in the English classroom.* New York, NY: Teachers College Press.

Rowe, M. B. (1976). Wait time and rewards as instructional variables, their influence on language, logic and fate control. *Journal of Research in Science Teaching, 11*(5), 81–94.

Scott, P. H., Mortimer, E. F., & Aguiar, O. G. (2006). The tension between authoritative and dialogic discourse: A fundamental characteristic of meaning making interactions in high school science lessons. *Science Education, 90*(4), 605–631.

Shepard, L. A. (2005, October). *Formative assessment: Caveat emptor.* Paper presented at ETS Invitational Conference, The Future of Assessment: Shaping Teaching and Learning, New York, NY.

Torrance, H., & Pryor, J. (1998). *Investigating formative assessment: Teaching, learning and assessment in the classroom.* Maidenhead, UK: McGraw-Hill Education.

CHAPTER

6

What Still Needs to Be Explored

Since its publication in 1998, *Inside the Black Box* by Paul Black and Dylan Wiliam has had a dramatic and positive effect on teaching and learning in many schools in many countries. Black and Wiliam's review presented teachers with a new way of thinking about the role of assessment—assessment for learning (AfL)—that changed the way that classrooms worked, allowing teachers to recognize, respond to, and improve learning. Its reach and popularity have stemmed from its rich, evidence-based practice approach.

In this book, we have explored how lines of research and practice associated with AfL ideas have developed and flourished in both the UK and the US over two decades. While there has been a good deal of similarity in the development overall in the two countries, the journeys have been differently driven and shaped by a range of policies and internal workings of each country. In this chapter, we attempt to summarize where we believe we have progressed with AfL practice, our better understanding of how and why it works across a range of contexts, and where we foresee further research and development is needed.

From Evidence-Based Practice to Practice-Based Evidence

Evidence-based education policies are high on the political agenda of many countries, which is not surprising given the rise of accountability in education systems in a number of them (Slavin, 2002). The term *evidence-based practice* (EBP) is now firmly entrenched in the education lexicon, and with good reason; improvements in student learning and educational outcomes depend on the wider use of reliable evidence in classroom practice. The evidence in question is supplied by research in response to both political and practical demands that educational research should contribute to practice.

The concept of EBP has its origins in medicine. It is sometimes known as the "what works" agenda, and its focus is on the use of the best available evidence to bring about desirable results. While often people think that EBP arises only from randomized controlled trials, it actually involves integrating individual clinical expertise with the best available external clinical evidence from systematic research (Sackett et al., 1996). The best research evidence is usually found in clinically relevant research that has been conducted using sound methodology (Sackett, 2002) and that is interpreted through accumulated clinical expertise. So in medicine, EBP is the integration of clinical expertise, patient values, and the best research evidence available to inform the decision-making process for patient care and treatment. Consequently, decisions are made using the evidence from rigorous and robust research that is then made sense of in the context of clinical practice.

Even though education is a different field from medicine, the ideas around robustness and rigor still hold, as well as the findings being used to make sense of practice. We explained in Chapter 1 that *Inside the Black Box* arose from a systematic review that included consideration of around fifty experimental studies that tested the effects of feedback on achievement, alongside over two hundred empirical and theoretical studies that informed how and why feedback is a key factor in supporting learning. What has followed from this small beginning is a vast experimentation of these ideas into practice, informed initially by the KMOFAP project (1999–2001) and then through sharing of evidence-based practice between practitioners, teacher educators, and researchers for the last twenty years.

James Gallagher in *Education Week* (2002) argued that evidence-based policies are setting up false expectations among policy makers because educational research is unlikely to produce miraculous breakthroughs like antibiotics did in medicine. However, the value of evidence-based policies does not always depend on breakthroughs, because some fields gradually make progressive, step-by-step, incremental improvements when they invest in research and development. This seems to have been the track taken by AfL; twenty years on, we know considerably more about what works and what doesn't, but more importantly, we understand the principles and have sufficient repertoires of practice to adapt to the range and growing diversity of our classrooms in both the UK and the US.

Perhaps the central point, though, is that new questions have arisen over these twenty years, some related to AfL's basic principles and others to its efficacy across a wider range of contexts, which, in turn, has stimulated further research and exploration of the evidence on which AfL's benefit to learning is based. While many teachers are introduced to research ideas in their preservice programs, experienced teachers also need to consult research to help them make sense of their growing understanding of effective pedagogy. As a result, we now have a growing bank of practice-based evidence where vignettes and reflections on practice have informed both the practitioner and research field. Such evidence provides teachers with illustrations of how AfL functions in practice that allows them to understand better how assessment can be embedded into teaching and learning, while alerting them to the types of thinking, planning, and ways of responding they need to consider to ensure AfL works in their own classrooms. The continued endeavor and focus on practice-based evidence has made AfL stand out from a research perspective and succeed as an approach to teaching and learning that is both workable and informative in the classroom.

Development of AfL

After twenty years, we remain convinced that AfL is a useful and profitable way of supporting learning in the classroom. AfL enables teachers to help children to learn and to learn how to learn.

Through the ongoing evidence of learning that AfL pedagogy provides, both teachers and their students know how they are doing in their current learning and what is needed next to take their learning forward. AfL provides both a purpose to teaching and a connection to what teachers do, and plan to do next, with how students are learning. This makes AfL both pragmatic and prospective in that teachers recognize and acknowledge learning as it is happening and become aware of student needs, thus setting up the potential and drive for future learning.

> After twenty years, we remain convinced that AfL is a useful and profitable way of supporting learning in the classroom. AfL enables teachers to help children to learn and to learn how to learn.

In the next section, we highlight what we have learned from practice-based evidence since the publication of *Inside the Black Box*.

Teachers Need to Be Vigilant for Evidence

Possibly the greatest thing we have learned watching teachers use AfL in their teaching over the last twenty years is that they need to be vigilant for evidence of learning. Sometimes the evidence is not easy to predict. An example might help here. Chris remembers Dylan Wiliam telling the story of his young niece, who was working on addition by placing groups of red and blue counters into a cup and then figuring out the total number of counters. The child showed her teacher the answer she had written down and was asked to show how she had worked it out. The child sat down and drew a picture of herself with a furrowed brow because she was quite mathematically capable for her age and had thought out the answer. The teacher had expected her to draw the five blue and the four red counters and then to count that there were nine counters in total. This child, however, did not need that particular mathematics strategy to get to the answer. This is evidence of learning; she had learned how to get there!

Interestingly, Chris saw a class doing a similar activity recently where the children were counting out a number of blue counters and a number of red counters into a pot and then tipping out all the counters and counting the total number of counters. The teacher noticed that one child was writing down six blue and three red as an answer instead of nine (counters). She sat with him and took him through the task. He carefully got to the end and counted nine counters. The teacher smiled and said, "So the answer is?" The boy answered, hesitatingly, "Six blue and three red." The teacher looked quizzical and asked, "Altogether?" The boy started to recount the counters and again decided on his "six blue and three red" answer. The teacher took the counters and demonstrated the task again, explaining each step she was taking, but the boy still looked doubtful when she concluded she had nine counters. He said, "But some are blue (counters) and some are red (counters). They are not the same." The counting strategy with red and blue counters was not helping this child's mathematical thinking.

The teacher went over to the fruit basket on her desk. (Most elementary schools in the UK provide all the children a free fruit snack halfway through the morning.) She selected six apples and three pears and found a paper bag in her desk drawer. She repeated the counting task using the fruit. The boy accepted that six apples and three pears made nine pieces of fruit. The teacher reset his questions to do the same task as the other children, but using fruit rather than counters. Through noticing what was inhibiting his learning, the teacher was able to work out how she might help him engage with the correct ways of thinking. By the end of the activity, the boy was able to work out, in his head, the total number of fruit and just used the final count as a check on his thinking. If the teacher had not intervened and responded to the needs of the child at that point, he would have finished the activity demotivated and unsure of what he was supposed to be doing. Also, if the teacher had left out checking in on how he was doing during the lesson, she might have thought he was poor at math, when in fact he managed to do good computational thinking because she had supported him initially. In both these scenarios about using counters to develop computational skills of addition, the evidence of learning was not what either teacher expected, but their assessment, judgment, and response enabled them to tailor the next steps in learning for each of these two students.

Teacher noticing through an AfL lens requires a sensitivity to the learning potential of student ideas, actions, and interactions. Experienced AfL teachers know their students well and have built up a detailed picture of how the children have learned in previous activities and so can, to some extent, have an awareness of where they need to support during a lesson or what resources or organization of students into groups might help specific learners. Recognizing where there is evidence of learning and also what specifically is inhibiting learning is sometimes hard to achieve in a busy classroom. However, good AfL teachers remain vigilant, using both observation of children as they undertake tasks and listening in to classroom conversations to try to identify how learning is progressing and where support might be needed. It is these noticing skills that enable teachers to develop their practice so they become more sensitive to the implications of student actions and the possibilities for acting creatively in the moment (Cowie, Harrison, & Willis, 2018).

Interactions Work in a Nuanced and Detailed Way

The second thing we have learned about AfL practice is that interactions that have a formative purpose work in a nuanced and detailed way in supporting learning. We witnessed this in Chapter 3 when the science teacher changed the language he was using in whole-class discussion activities to encourage the learners to focus on and value thinking. Gradually, the learners in this class demonstrated that they were thinking more and developing their ideas, as well as adopting similar language to that of the teacher in their responses. In some lessons, we have seen teachers provide alternative answers to a question and ask the students, "*So what do you think?*" However, previously they might have asked, "*So which is correct?*" This change in language and move toward more purposeful interactions enculture students into ways of thinking that encourage them to take an active role in learning, which supports them in sharing their ideas with others. Through a more open approach to student ideas and a willingness to learn from others and from one's own mistakes, the AfL classroom provides an environment that helps children learn how to learn.

Context Matters

The third piece of learning about AfL pedagogy is that context matters and teachers need to adopt and adapt AfL practices to fit their subject discipline, their learners, and their environment. The ability to adapt AfL practice begins with planning for learning, as explained in Chapter 4, and requires teachers to transform the ways they work with learners in the classroom, as we documented in Chapter 5. Also, in Chapter 4 we looked at the importance of professional learning communities in helping teachers develop and progress their AfL pedagogy, highlighting the need for professional learning in a context that is supported by colleagues. These ways of professional thinking related to AfL have only arisen in the last decade and have been promoted through particular groups who have sustained an interest in AfL, such as the Council of Chief State School Officers' Formative Assessment State Collaborative (FAST SCASS) in the US and the Association for Science Education and other professional subject groups in the UK.

The focus on AfL within the research field has centered around teacher practices, and while some researchers have also explored the learner's perspective (Alton-Lee & Nuthall, 1995; Cowie, 2005; Nuthall, 2007), the major moves in AfL research have focused on teachers and their practice. Students' conceptions of the role AfL plays on their learning is clearly an area that needs further development, and some movement has been made in AfL thinking more recently. We pick up on this in the next few sections.

Learning Identity

Since the publication of *Inside the Black Box*, some work has explored the development of students' learning identity in the context of AfL (e.g., Heritage & Wylie, 2018; Stobart, 2008) and some promising avenues of practice have opened up, but this remains a topic that is both undertheorized and under-researched. Because a learning identity is so important to being a successful learner both in school and through life, we propose this as an area that needs to be explored further.

Learning identity is a key aspect of metacognitive knowledge about how one learns; people with a learning identity see themselves as learners and believe in their ability to learn. A learning identity develops over time and can be nurtured in school so that eventually students acquire a learning self-identity that permeates all aspects of their life, in and outside of school.

> Learning identity is a key aspect of metacognitive knowledge about how one learns; people with a learning identity see themselves as learners and believe in their ability to learn. A learning identity develops over time and can be nurtured in school so that eventually students acquire a learning self-identity that permeates all aspects of their life, in and outside of school.

It is worth reiterating here the importance of students developing competencies for lifelong learning that we have addressed in previous chapters and to underscore the significance of a learning identity to continued learning throughout life.

In Chapter 3, we introduced the idea of "mindsets" that arose from Carol Dweck's (2008) research: People who have a "fixed mindset" believe that intelligence is fixed, whereas those with a "growth mindset" believe that intellectual ability can develop. To varying degrees, those with a "fixed mindset" believe that they are incapable of learning (Molden & Dweck, 2006). For example, some people believe they cannot do mathematics, so they don't learn to do mathematics, whereas those with a stronger learning identity in mathematics bring a more confident learning orientation to learning the subject and are willing to persevere with challenging tasks (cf. Zimmerman, 2000).

Teachers' AfL practices can shape students' learning identity in several ways. First, when teachers are responding to students' emerging ideas in ways that ensure the students are consistently on the "edge" of their learning (Heritage & Heritage, 2013), all students can make progress from where they are to where they can go next. At the risk of stating the obvious, when students' ideas are respected and when they experience consistent progress (with difficulties, challenges, and misconceptions surmounted along the way), they can feel successful as learners—they know they can learn.

Second, in AfL, teachers are not looking for the "right" or "wrong" in student responses; they are looking to make sense of how students are thinking about a topic so they can take pedagogical action, including providing focused feedback that assists students to move their own learning closer to meeting the intended goal. Feedback that teachers provide in AfL is much more effective in supporting learning identities than simply telling students if they are right or wrong. It is also more beneficial to the development of a learning identity than grading practices that abound in so many schools, which make only some students winners and imply a permanent lack of ability for others when learning goals appear out of reach (Shepard, 2019).

And third, students can develop learning identities through active reflection of what it means to be a learner. AfL provides teachers with opportunities to engage students in meaningful self-assessment through which they ask themselves what worked in their learning, what strategies they can adopt in similar learning situations, and what strategies they might need to try next.

Students' learning identity is also shaped by their perceptions of how others view them as learners. In this regard, students need to learn in an identity-safe environment (Steele & Cohn-Vargas, 2013). Further exploration of the development of learner identity through AfL will also require more research and practice-based evidence on how the classroom culture shapes identity in positive ways.

Identity-Safe Environments

Consider a classroom in which there are several students who are learning English at the same time as they are learning subject matter content. The English learner students (ELs) try to use their limited English in responding to questions or engaging in discussions with their peers. However, their efforts are met with responses from the teacher and their peers that indicate they are not willing to try to make sense of the ideas that are being communicated and do not value their contributions. Contrast this situation with a classroom in which the teacher does not permit EL students' "flawed" language (Valdés, 2005) to inhibit either his or his students' comprehension of EL students' communication, nor prevent ELs' participation in collaborative work with their English-speaking peers. It will be evident which classroom is an identity-safe environment. In such an environment, the teacher works to ensure that students feel their identity is an asset and not a barrier to success at school and that who they are and what they think matters (Steele & Cohn-Vargas, 2013).

We have seen in previous chapters how interaction is central to learning and to AfL. Teachers and peers have access to student thinking from the discussions and question-and-answer sessions they engage in together. However, students decide whether or not to participate in interactions depending on the classroom dynamic and their past experience with their peers and their teachers. The more that students trust their peers, the more likely they are ready to take the risks necessary to learn (James, Kobe, & Zhao, 2017). It is not hard to imagine, for instance, in the first classroom example given that EL students would quickly get the message that the classroom is not a safe place for them to reveal either their language competence or their thinking. An identity-safe environment is a community of practice characterized by norms of collaboration, trust, and an appreciation of differences, in which students can take joint responsibility for learning (Heritage, 2013, 2016). Such norms are prerequisites for the development of learning identities, and we propose that more work is needed to investigate ways in which the classroom culture and the learning relationships within it impact the development of a learning identity.

One aspect to creating an identity-safe environment in which a learning identity is supported is the inclusion of students' "funds of knowledge" within learning and assessment.

Funds of Knowledge

We know that students' prior knowledge in a discipline is important to build on in developing new learning. In a sociocultural approach to teaching and learning that we discussed in Chapter 3, students' prior knowledge includes not just the academic knowledge they have acquired, but also the knowledge that they bring from their homes and communities—their "funds of knowledge."

The term *funds of knowledge* is derived from Louis Moll and colleagues who studied the knowledge found within working-class, Mexican communities in Tucson, Arizona, for the purpose of developing innovations in teaching that draw on the knowledge and skills found in local households (Moll, Amanti, Neff, & Gonzalez, 1992). Their research recognized that, in the main, teachers only know the individuals they teach as "students" from their performance within the classroom contexts rather than knowing them as a "whole person" from a home-based context. In a classroom where teaching and learning are characterized by sociocultural approaches, students enter the learning community as a "whole person," and their participation between home and school is mediated by the members of the community as they acquire "school knowledge."

Moll and colleagues advocated drawing on students' funds of knowledge not to merely reproduce household knowledge in the classroom but rather to legitimize students' experience as valid and to build on the familiar knowledge bases that students can manipulate to enhance learning in subject matter content in school (González, 2006). In essence, this means using students' knowledge acquired in their homes and communities in ways that enhance "students' sense of themselves as knowledge-makers and knowers" (Cowie et al., 2018, p. 7).

One question that we think is important to explore further is how teachers can leverage students' "funds of knowledge" within AfL to promote learning. What teachers see their students do in classroom learning tasks may not reflect what they are capable of doing (James et al., 2017). For this reason, it is important to investigate the degree to which bringing students' funds of knowledge to engage in learning tasks provides greater insights for teachers into their thinking and what they are actually capable of doing, and also the degree to which feedback that leverages students' funds of knowledge is beneficial to securing students' progress. Some groups have already begun to explore these ideas. For example, in the United States, members of the state collaborative mentioned in Chapter 2, the FAST SCASS, have devoted a considerable amount of time to thinking about the connections between funds of knowledge and AfL. Although the group's ideas are very preliminary, the members have begun the exploration that we encourage others to pursue.

> *It is important to investigate the degree to which bringing students' funds of knowledge to engage in learning tasks provides greater insights for teachers into their thinking and what they are actually capable of doing.*

The previous section focused on teachers' knowledge about their students for learning and assessment. In what follows, we address another source of knowledge teachers need for teaching and that we believe is important to explore further in terms of its contribution to effective AfL practices.

Disciplinary Knowledge

In Chapter 4, we pointed to a resurgence of interest in the disciplinary nature of AfL since *Inside the Black Box* was published (e.g., Andrade, Bennett, & Cizek, 2019) and discussed how teachers' disciplinary knowledge might form the bedrock for richer AfL practices. Teachers' disciplinary knowledge goes beyond having knowledge and skills to do mathematics or write an effective essay; it requires knowledge for teaching (Ball, Thames, & Phelps, 2008). In this regard, Lee Shulman (1987) identified a particular kind of knowledge that teachers need for teaching, which he referred to as pedagogical content knowledge (PCK), "the special amalgam between content and pedagogy" (p. 7) needed for teaching a particular subject. Building on Shulman's ideas, researchers have since elaborated the concept of pedagogical content knowledge and shown how teaching demands a simultaneous integration of key ideas in the discipline with the ways in which students understand them (Ball et al., 2008).

Less attention has been paid to the importance of teachers' PCK for assessment, specifically for AfL, although the idea of PCK has been raised in connection with teachers' use of assessment information. For example, an investigation that Margaret and her colleagues conducted into how teachers used assessment information to decide on students' next learning steps found that the overwhelming majority of teachers in their study had difficulty knowing what to do next, and they hypothesized that a major reason for that was their lack of PCK (Heritage, Kim, Vendlinski, & Herman, 2009). For instance, it seems self-evident that to respond to students' emerging ideas, teachers require knowledge of the ways in which students think when engaging with specific topics within a discipline, and they need knowledge of instructional strategies so that they can orchestrate many complex judgments in the course of a lesson about appropriate and immediate actions intended to advance learning.

Further exploration by teachers and researchers will be needed to shed light on the contribution of teachers' disciplinary knowledge, specifically their PCK, to AfL and to tease out the nuances, if any, between PCK for teaching and PCK for assessment.

The past twenty years of AfL implementation have provided us with a greater breadth and depth of understanding of its contribution to many facets of student learning. We have aimed to highlight these facets throughout the book. We have also pointed to some future directions that we believe are important to explore with a view to making AfL an even more robust factor in the development of all students' learning. Some still need to be convinced of the benefits of AfL to student learning as a result of more research studies that demonstrate improved performance on academic outcome measures. While we agree that research of that kind is important, we worry that focusing solely on outcome measures misses the wealth of benefits that AfL affords both teaching and learning.

At a time when countries' education systems and jurisdictions are considering the knowledge, skills, values, and attitudes that today's students need to thrive and shape their world (OECD, 2018), we firmly believe that AfL needs to be part of that conversation. So many instances in our respective countries have convinced us that AfL can assist students in developing the agency, competencies, and the sense of purpose they need to shape their own lives and contribute to the lives of others (OECD, 2018). In this regard, we look forward to witnessing how the AfL story continues to unfold in the years to come.

REFERENCES

Alton-Lee, A. G., & Nuthall, G. A., with Patrick, J. (1995). Reframing classroom research: A lesson from the private world of children. In G. Capella Noya, K. Geismar, & G. Nicoleau (Eds.), *Shifting histories: Transforming education for social change*. Cambridge, MA: Harvard Educational Review. Reprint series No. 26.

Andrade, H. L., Bennett, R. E., & Cizek, G. J. (Eds.). (2019). *Handbook of formative assessment in the disciplines*. New York, NY: Routledge.

Ball, D. L., Thames, M. H., & Phelps, G. (2008). Content knowledge for teaching. *Journal of Teacher Education, 59*(5), 389–407.

Cowie, B. (2005). Pupil commentary on assessment for learning. *The Curriculum Journal, (16)*2, 137–151.

Cowie, B., Harrison, C., & Willis, J. (2018). Supporting teacher responsiveness in assessment for learning through disciplined noticing. *The Curriculum Journal, 29*(4), 464–478.

Dweck, C. S. (2008). *Mindset: The new psychology of success*. New York, NY: Random House Digital.

Gallagher, J. (2002). What next for OERI? *Education Week, 21*(28), 52.

González, N. (2006). Beyond culture: The hybridity of funds of knowledge. In N. González, L. C. Moll, & C. Amanti (Eds.), *Funds of knowledge: Theorizing practices in households, communities, and classrooms* (pp. 41–58). New York, NY: Routledge.

Heritage, M. (2013). *Formative assessment: A process of inquiry and action*. Cambridge, MA: Harvard Education Press.

Heritage, M. (2016). Assessment for learning: Co-regulation in and as student–teacher interaction. In *Assessment for learning: Meeting the challenge of implementation* (pp. 327–343). Cham, Switzerland: Springer.

Heritage, M., & Heritage, J. (2013). Teacher questioning: The epicenter of instruction and assessment. *Applied Measurement in Education, 26*(3), 176–190.

Heritage, M., Kim, J., Vendlinski, T., & Herman, J. (2009). From evidence to action: A seamless process in formative assessment? *Educational Measurement: Issues and Practice, 28*(3), 24–31.

Heritage, M., & Wylie, C. (2018). Reaping the benefits of assessment for learning: Achievement, identity, and equity. *ZDM, 50*(4), 729–741.

James, J. H., Kobe, J., & Zhao, X. (2017). Examining the role of trust in shaping children's approaches to peer dialogue. *Teachers College Record, 119*(10), 1–34.

Molden, D. C., & Dweck, C. S. (2006). Finding "meaning" in psychology: A lay theories approach to self-regulation, social perception, and social development. *American Psychologist, 61*(3), 192.

Moll, L. C., Amanti, C., Neff, D., & Gonzalez, N. (1992). Funds of knowledge for teaching: Using a qualitative approach to connect homes and classrooms. *Theory Into Practice, 31*(2), 132–141.

Nuthall, G. (2007). *Hidden lives of learners*. Wellington, New Zealand: NZCER Press.

Organisation for Economic Co-operation and Development. (2018). *The future of education and skills: Education 2030*. Paris, France: OECD.

Sackett, D. L. (2002). The arrogance of preventive medicine. *Canadian Medical Association Journal, 167*, 363–364.

Sackett, D. L., Rosenberg, W. M., Gray, J. A., Haynes, R. B., & Richardson, W. S. (1996). Evidence-based medicine: What it is and what it isn't. *British Medical Journal, 312*, 71–72.

Shepard, L. A. (2019). Classroom assessment to support teaching and learning. In A. Berman, M. J. Feuer, & J. W. Pellegrino (Eds.), *The Annals of the American Academy of Political and Social Science* (pp. 183–200). Thousand Oaks, CA: SAGE.

Shulman, L. S. (1987). Knowledge and teaching: Foundations of the new reform. *Harvard Educational Review, 57*, 1–22.

Slavin, R. E. (2002). Evidence-based education policies: Transforming educational practice and research. *Educational Researcher, 31*(7), 15–21.

Steele, D. M., & Cohn-Vargas, B. (2013). *Identity-safe classrooms: Places to belong and learn.* Thousand Oaks, CA: Corwin.

Stobart, G. (2008). *Testing times: The uses and abuses of assessment.* London, UK: Routledge.

Valdés, G. (2005). Bilingualism, heritage language learners, and SLA research: Opportunities lost or seized? *The Modern Language Journal, 89*, 410–426.

Zimmerman, B. J. (2000). Self-efficacy: An essential motive to learn. *Contemporary Educational Psychology, 25*(1), 82–91.

Index

Figures and notes are indicated by f or n following the page number.

Practice-based evidence, 106–107
Praise, 63–64
Prior knowledge, 112–113
Professional learning, 80
Professional learning communities, 80–83, 109
Progressions, 79
Progress versus performance, 64

Questioning
    classroom dialogue and, 38–41
    in KMOFAP project, 26–27
    language use, 109
    strengthening of, 95–98
    student role in, 9–10
Quizzes, 92

Reay, Diane, 24–25
Responsive teaching, 32
Revision, 27–28
Routines, 9–10, 101–103

Safety, 8, 101, 111–112
SATs (standardized assessment tasks), 21
Scrutiny of teaching plans, 90
Self-assessment, 30–31, 42–45, 43f, 94, 111
Self-esteem, 10
Self-helplessness, 64
Self-regulated learning, 57–62, 65
Shepard, Lorrie, 33–34, 37, 78
Shulman, Lee, 113
Sociocultural perspective, 52–57
Spenceley, Paul, 82–83
Standardized assessment tasks (SATs), 21
Standards, 5–7, 36–37, 36n, 71, 76–77, 81
Standards for Professional Learning, 81
State education agencies (SEAs), 34–35
Stiggins, Rick, 33
Student experiences, 54–55
Student response to teacher feedback strategy, 29, 95
Student role
    Black and Wiliam and, 51, 101
    as constructors of learning, 70–71, 99–100
    feedback and, 15

learning identity and, 110–111
    questioning and, 9–10
    teacher language choice and, 56–57
Study skills, 58
Systematic review versus meta-analysis, 2–3

Task Group on Assessment and Testing (TGAT), 20–21
A Taxonomy for Teaching, Learning, and Assessment (Anderson et al.), 96–97
Teacher learning communities (TLC), 80–83, 109
Teacher role, 19
Teacher talk, 98–99
Teaching versus learning, 83, 89–90, 102–103
Tests, 92
Think, Pair, Share, 27
Tierney, R. D., 53
Traffic Lighting, 94–95
Transmission model of learning, 69, 70, 93, 102–103
Two Stars and a Wish strategy, 30

Understanding, 96–97
United Kingdom
    assessment practices historically, 17–21
    Assessment Reform Group in, 4, 21–23
    effects of changing assessment priorities, 23–26
    evolution of assessment for learning practice, 26–31
    obstacles to implementation of assessment for learning, 31–32
    planning for learning and, 83
    policy decisions and, 77–78
    similarities with US, 45
United States
    changes in practice, 38–45
    development of assessment for learning, 33–35
    history and context, 32–33
    obstacles to implementation of assessment for learning, 35–36
    planning for learning and, 83–84

A SAGE Publishing Company

Helping educators make the greatest impact

CORWIN HAS ONE MISSION: to enhance education through intentional professional learning.

We build long-term relationships with our authors, educators, clients, and associations who partner with us to develop and continuously improve the best evidence-based practices that establish and support lifelong learning.